VIKING AGE
ENGLAND

VIKING AGE ENGLAND

JULIAN D. RICHARDS

First published by B.T. Batsford/English Heritage 1991

First published by Tempus 2000
This edition published 2007

Reprinted in 2010 by
The History Press
The Mill, Brimscombe Mill,
Stroud, Gloucestershire, GL5 2QG
www.thehistorypress.co.uk

Reprinted 2012, 2014

British Library Cataloguing in Publication Data.
A catalogue record for this book is available from the British Library.

ISBN 978 0 7524 2888 8

Typesetting and origination by Tempus Publishing
Printed and bound in Great Britain

CONTENTS

PREFACE AND ACKNOWLEDGEMENTS

This book is the substantially revised 2000 version of the volume first published in the Batsford/English Heritage series in 1991. In 2000 I took the opportunity to rewrite sections I was not happy with and to update the text in order to reflect new discoveries and shifting interpretations. This 2004 edition is unaltered apart from some changes to the format and layout.

The present book still relies upon the often unacknow-ledged labours of large numbers of archaeologists and others. I am especially grateful, however, to a smaller number from whom I have benefited from specific discussion, including Martin Biddle and Birthe Kjølbye-Biddle, Justine Bayley, Martin Carver, Dawn Hadley, Richard Hall, James Graham-Campbell, the late Jim Lang, Neil Price, David Stocker and Steve Roskams. To each of them, and to all those I haven't mentioned by name, thank you for your help. Where you have saved me from errors I am especially grateful, but where mistakes remain they are, of course, my own responsibility.

Many people and organisations have generously allowed me to make use of drawings and photographs, and they also retain the copyright, as acknowledged in the captions. Many of the black and white line drawings for the first edition were prepared by Dawn Flower at the English Heritage Drawing Office. Additional drawings are by Chris Philo and Stephanie Wood.

I

THE VIKING AGE

This book is about the development of Anglo-Saxon England from AD 800 until the Norman Conquest. For almost 250 years England was subject to attacks from Scandinavia. Contemporary chroniclers called the raiders by many names, including heathens and pagans, as well as Northmen and Danes, but one of the names used to refer to them by the English was 'Viking', and this is now used to describe not only the raiders, but also the period during which they carried out their attacks. These centuries, from the ninth to the eleventh, have become known, therefore, as the Viking Age.

The Vikings themselves can be elusive. The introduction of Scandinavian art styles can be seen on jewellery and sculpture, but Scandinavian-style houses and graves are often difficult to identify. Indeed, the relationship between Scandinavian settlers and the existing population must be considered to see how far the newcomers adopted native customs or invented new ones, sometimes rendering themselves indistinguishable from the local people and invisible to the archaeologist; sometimes creating new identities. This story will focus, therefore, on the period rather than on the people, and will examine all the archaeological traces of Viking Age England. It will be concerned particularly with England where, as a result of major excavations conducted over the last 30 years in towns like York, Lincoln and London, and in the countryside at sites such as Goltho, Raunds and Wharram Percy, we may now be closer to understanding the nature of Scandinavian interaction with the local population. Scotland, the Northern Isles, and the areas bordering the Irish Sea were also subject to separate Scandinavian influence, but are outside the scope of this book. The Scottish Hebrides and the Isle of Man were settled as a Norse kingdom of Man and the Western Isles. They formed part of an important axis between the Hiberno-Norse of Dublin and the Anglo-Scandinavian kings of York. The Isle of Man maintains elements of its Norse heritage to the present day, including the tradition of meetings of the Viking assembly or *Thing* in an annual open-air meeting of the Manx Parliament, the Tynwald. Nonetheless both Scotland and the Isle of Man have been the subject of several recent books, and Scandinavian settlement there will only be considered in relation to developments in England.

Two themes run through this book. Firstly, what was the Scandinavian contribution to the development of Late Saxon England? How far did the newcomers simply modify local developments already in progress? Was there anything distinctive about Scandinavian settlements? Were the major trading towns, such as Jorvik, already established before Scandinavian traders arrived? What was the Scandinavian influence on the formation of the English state?

Secondly, we shall take up the question of Scandinavian and native interaction. What was the native response to Scandinavians in the areas settled? What was it about the Scandinavian character that meant that in some areas, such as the Danelaw, they disappeared, fusing with the local traditions; whilst in others, such as the Isle of Man, they preserved a distinctive culture. How did they adapt, both economically, and in social and religious terms, to local circumstances? We need to bear in mind that interaction between the two peoples would have been subject to a number of factors: the extent of social, economic and political dependence of one group on the other, the ability of people to talk with one another, the degree of intermarriage, or of cultural and religious assimilation. We must also bear in mind that this was a long and complex process, spanning three hundred years, with much local variation.

THE VIKINGS YESTERDAY AND TODAY

The precise derivation of the term 'Viking' remains obscure. In Old Icelandic a *vik* was a bay or creek, and may have given its name to those sea-faring raiders who lurked in bays and estuaries. Vik is also the name of the area around the Oslofjord, and may have been used to describe anyone from that area of southern Norway. The Old Icelandic verb *vikya*, on the other hand, meant 'to turn aside' and may have been used to describe those away from home. In the Icelandic Sagas *víkingr* came to be used as a noun to refer to a warrior, or pirate, *víking* was used to refer to an expedition.

The majority of Scandinavians, therefore, were not Vikings; only those who went *a-viking* could really qualify for the description.

The first occurrence of *wicing* in Old English refers to Mediterranean pirates who may not even have been Scandinavians, centuries before the Viking Age. The term does not appear to have been used exclusively to refer to raiders from Scandinavia until the tenth century, under the influence of the Viking invasions. There are only five occurrences of *wicings* in the Anglo-Saxon Chronicle (Fell 1986; 1987), and each time the word seems to be used in connection with a small group of raiders, rather than an army. Its use appears to have died out during the Middle Ages, until it was reintroduced in the Romantic era and it was only during the nineteenth century that 'Viking' became the standard term for Scandinavian invaders.

Three men popularised Vikings outside Scandinavia. Richard Wagner completed the Ring cycle in 1874, using stories derived from the Edda and Sagas to erect a pastiche of Germanic mythology. Wagner introduced a number of popular misconceptions including winged and horned helmets, which probably originated as theatrical costume design. In Britain Walter Scott developed an interest in the Norse history of Scotland, publishing his novel *The Pirate* in 1822, followed by a series of popular children's adventure stories (Wilson 1996). Finally, William Morris and other members of the pre-Raphaelite movement were attracted by Scandinavian romanticism. Morris developed a passion for medieval Scandinavia whilst an undergraduate at Oxford. He went on to learn Old Icelandic and helped translate a number of sagas, travelling in Iceland in 1871 and 1873. One of the first to take an interest in the material evidence of the Viking Age in England was W.G. Collingwood, Ruskin's secretary and biographer. Collingwood's association with Morris stimulated his interest in Anglo-Saxons and Vikings; he devoted the last 30 years of his life to a study of stone sculpture, eventually published in 1927 as *Northumbrian crosses of the pre-Norman Age*.

During the nineteenth century Anglo-Saxon and Old Norse were developed as university subjects on a par with the classical languages, but apparently maintained a class association: chairs of Scandinavian Studies were often founded by northern industrialists (Wawn 2000). In general, when Vikings were mentioned by English historians, they appeared as villainous barbarians, and as foils for the great hero King Ælfred. Although the Viking Age was equated with nobility of adventure and exploration, and it was quite acceptable for Viking settlers in Iceland to be seen as founders of democracy and respectable exponents of nationalism, in Victorian England it was the Anglo-Saxons who were seen as the ancestral English.

For most English historians the Scandinavian settlement was largely discounted and ignored. Unlike the arrival of three boatloads of Anglo-Saxon mercenaries it could not be presented as the birth of the English race; unlike the Norman Conquest it could not be seen as a major constitutional change. Most significantly, the Vikings in England failed to produce their own historian; their deeds are known solely through the eyes of West Saxon chroniclers, and so long as modern commentators patriotically continued to echo the views of those chroniclers, the Vikings were guaranteed short shrift (Trafford 2000).

In Nazi Germany theVikings were put to a more sinister use (Müller-Wille 1996). The Nazis identified with the so-called Aryan people of Scandinavia. Vikings became part of the fair-haired, blue-eyed, clean-living ideal of the German National Socialist Party. At its most extreme Nazism intended to replace Christianity with the old paganism of the Germanic gods. During the 1930s, excavations of the early Schleswig town at Hedeby were backed by the German state apparatus, which wished to emphasise a unity with the people of Scandinavia which had little foundation in reality. The Norwegian National Socialist party used the barrow cemetery at Borre, Vestfold, in Norway, as a backdrop for its political rallies from 1935-44. The assembled throng was told that:

> We gather here because the people who united Norway in one kingdom were buried here. These people carried the name of Norway all over the world. It was these people who founded states in Russia and, in a certain sense, also the British Empire.

English history since the Second World War has been dominated by an emphasis on the Germanic invasions of England. The influence of Scandinavians has been particularly prominent, supported by a reliance on place-name studies, although with few grave finds there has been little role for archaeology in traditional interpretations of Viking settlement. This interpretation was challenged by Peter Sawyer in *The Age of the Vikings*, which has struck a chord with archaeologists who now tend to downplay the role of population movement and emphasise local developments. More recently, scholars have argued that material culture and language should not be read as a passive reflection of Anglo-Saxons and Vikings, but as tools to be used actively in the integration of settlers and indigenous inhabitants and in the construction of new identities (Hadley and Richards 2000). This is beginning to focus attention away from the irresolvable problem of numbers and onto issues of identity which may be explored with reference to linguistic and archaeological evidence.

On the other hand, the popular vision remains loosely the same as it was in the late nineteenth century. In the popular press Vikings remain a stereotype for rape and pillage; at weekends people dress up in Viking costume and re-enact their battles; Vikings are a major crowd-puller.

VIKINGS IN ENGLAND

In general, contemporary western European texts referred to Vikings as *Dani*, or Danes, and *Nordmanni*, or Northmen, irrespective of their country of origin. No doubt to the English they all sounded the same, but it is also not clear that nationality was a meaningful distinction anyway, as the various Scandinavian states were only formed during the Viking Age. At first, the Scandinavians thought of themselves as inhabitants of particular regions, such as men of Jutland, Vestfold, Hordaland and so on. As a sense of national identity grew, so did the use of national names. Ohthere, a Scandinavian visitor to Ælfred's court, distinguished between Norwegians, Swedes and Danes.

Certainly, we know that Viking armies comprised warriors of various races, just as modern mercenary armies do. The armies that attacked England in the reign of Æthelstan included men from eastern Sweden as well as from Norway and Denmark, although the English identified them by their leaders, as armies of Olafr, Sveinn, Thorkel or Knutr, and thought of them all as Danes. The loyalty of Viking warriors would have been to their leaders, rather than to any national identity. In Ireland, Danes and Norwegians fought each other, and in 838 the Britons of Devon and Cornwall formed an alliance with the Danes against the West Saxons under King Ecgbryht.

By their customs and appearance Viking settlers would initially have appeared foreign to native Anglo-Saxons. Scandinavian jewellery was unlike that of the Anglo-Saxons. Norse settlers imported the ring-headed pin from Celtic Ireland, and presumably the Irish style of cloak that went with it. They wore silver arm rings as symbols of their wealth. The men may have worn belted trousers, without covering tunics, unlike the Anglo-Saxons who wore leggings and tunics. When the Vikings first appeared their hair was worn shaved, short at the back and shaggy at the front; imitation of this style was condemned by the Church. By the time of the Domesday Book Viking-descended Normans still wore their hair shaved up the nape; the English wore their hair long, and were sneered at by the Normans for effeminacy.

Some settlers must have brought their wives with them; when the Anglo-Saxons stormed Benfleet they captured goods, women and children. Viking women also followed fashions different from those of the Anglo-Saxons. They wore a bow brooch on each shoulder, for instance, and a trefoil brooch at the centre. Other Vikings presumably intermarried

with native women. A later chronicler said that the success of
Vikings with Anglo-Saxon women was due to the fact that
they bathed on Saturdays, combed their hair, and wore fine
clothing.

For how long were the separate identities maintained?
Certain laws of Æthelred and Edgar demonstrate that there
was a distinction between Danes and Anglo-Saxons in the
second half of the tenth century, but the term 'Danelaw' was
not used until 1008. Knutr recognised or permitted differences between Danes and their customs, and the English and
theirs. Because they had money to buy farms and settle, and
because they remained 'foreigners', Danish families may have
met with resentment and prejudice; Æthelred spoke of them
as having 'sprung up in this island, sprouting like poisonous
weeds among the wheat'. But were Danish settlers preserving
a strong sense of their identity? The Scandinavian settlement was not a single event. Throughout the tenth century
there would have been continued contact with Scandinavia
through trade, and arrivals of new groups of Scandinavian
mercenaries. In 1016 there was a fresh influx of settlers
under Knutr. There is no evidence for any feeling of Danish
national identity which motivated local action and caused the
Danes to act as a group in areas of dispute or in support of
rival claimants to the throne. Epigraphical evidence suggests
that in England at least, Scandinavian settlers quickly dropped
their native language and spoke English.

Tenth- and eleventh-century observers might speak of
the Danelaw as a distinct political unit, but the definition of
political boundaries was more complex than racial divisions.
Political lordship and allegiance rather than Anglo-Saxon,
Celtic, Danish or Norse race were the determining factors

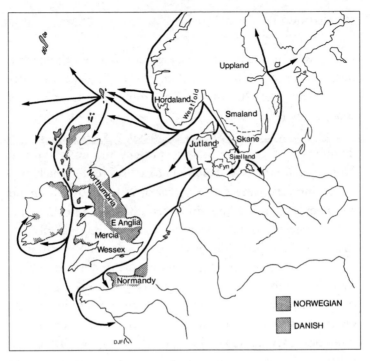

1 North-west Europe in the Viking Age

(Hadley 1997; Innes 2000). Despite recent advances in DNA research, genetic evidence is of little help in trying to identify Vikings. It is impossible to say, on genetic grounds, whether an individual was from Scandinavia, although some genetic evidence can plausibly be interpreted as reflecting a general Scandinavian influx in areas such as north-east Derbyshire and Cumbria where the gene frequencies are close to those on parts of Scandinavia (Evison 2000).

SCANDINAVIA

It is possible to make some generalisations about the peoples involved in the Viking settlement in England, as their movements were inevitably determined by Scandinavian topography (*1*).

The Norwegians have always been a sea-faring people. Thousands of offshore islands protect the west coast of Norway and provide a sheltered coastal sea route which gives the country its name, the *Norvegur* or North Way. Mountains rise steeply from the fjord-indented coastline, and the population is mostly confined to narrow ledges and small plains at the head of the fjords. There were no towns in Norway at the beginning of the Viking Age, although several had developed by its end. From the seventh century it has been suggested that the population of Norway was expanding; by the eighth century there is evidence for the emergence of petty kingdoms (Myhre 1998). The population grew first up the valleys and into the forest areas, but increasingly the Norse looked to the west. From the 980s the country entered an expansionist phase under Haraldr Fine-Hair, King of Vestfold; and from *c*.930 under his son, Erik Bloodaxe.

The first Viking raiders whose presence is recorded in the British Isles were probably Norse. During the reign of Beorhtric (786-802) 'there came for the first time three ships of Northmen from Hordaland and then the reeve rode to them and wished to force them to the king's residence, for he did not know what they were; and they slew him. Those were the first ships of Danish men which came to the land of the English.' Despite the confusion, it seems likely that the ships were from Norway because of the specific reference to

Hordaland; the last sentence was probably added as a gloss by a later writer when the Danes were seen as the chief threat. Norse warriors must also have joined Knutr's eleventh-century army; a memorial stone was erected in Galteland, Aust Agder (Norway) by Arnsteinn in memory of his son Biorr who 'was killed in the guard when Knutr attacked England'.

Today, Denmark comprises the Jutland peninsula and the large islands of Fyn and Sjælland, plus some 500 smaller islands as well as Bornholm in the Baltic Sea. However, during the Viking Age it also included Skåne in southern Sweden. The southern frontier at the foot of the Jutland peninsula also lay further to the south, where from AD 737 it was defended by a series of earthworks known as the Danevirke. During the Viking Age Denmark was extensively wooded with oak and beech, but much of the landscape was wasteland, sand dunes and heath. Nowhere was more than 56km (35 miles) from the sea, which provided the basis of the livelihood of much of the population.

Denmark, and especially Jutland, was more affected by developments in western Europe than was the rest of Scandinavia. Early trading towns developed, such as those at Hedeby and Ribe, and organised central power emerged in the eighth century, at least in Jutland.

The first references to Danes are as pirates raiding the Carolingian empire. Danes naturally looked to the North Sea coast, plundering Frisian territory, such as the trading post at Dorestad. They continued west through the English Channel to raid France and southern England. The Danes were responsible for the main concerted raids on the British Isles in the ninth century and many of them settled in the Danelaw.

From the mid-tenth century we know of a continuous succession of kings, beginning with Gorm the Old. From the 960s royal power was extended under Gorm's son, Haraldr Bluetooth, who rebuilt the Danevirke, constructed a series of regional tax collection centres to a standard Trelleborg fortress design, declared Christianity the official religion of Denmark, and conquered Norway. Haraldr was ousted in 987; Gorm's grandson, Sveinn Forkbeard, and his great-grandson, Knutr, both led armies against England, the latter becoming king of England and Denmark from 1016 to 1035.

Sweden comprises a number of regions with local variations in soil, climate and relief. To the north of Skåne, the infertile and sparsely populated plateau of Småland formed a natural boundary with Denmark. Most of the people lived in the well-forested fertile zones in the central lowlands. To the north, Norrland was sparsely populated, consisting of forest and bare rock. Off the east coast the island of Gotland was of particular importance, occupying a strategic position at the centre of the Baltic. Baltic trade had made this area tremendously wealthy and its inhabitants had penetrated as far as Byzantium. Swedish Vikings continued to look mainly to the east, sailing down the great rivers into Russia; Sweden remained relatively isolated from developments in western Europe. Several kings are mentioned in association with Birka (near present day Stockholm) but the extent of their control is unknown; Sweden only emerged as a unified state in the course of the eleventh and twelfth centuries. There were comparatively few Swedish visitors to the British Isles although some southern Swedes must have served with Knutr; a rune stone from Väsby, Uppland, for example, records that 'Alle had this stone put up in his own honour. He took Knutr's *danegeld* in England. May God help his soul.'

ENGLAND AT THE BEGINNING OF THE VIKING AGE

By the mid-ninth century England still comprised four independent kingdoms: East Anglia, Wessex, Mercia and Northumbria. Mercia was the strongest military power, extending west to Offa's Dyke, the great earthwork constructed along its frontier with Wales, and south to the Thames. Northumbria was divided by internecine feuding between the rulers of Bernicia to the north, and Deira in the south, and its northern borders were troubled by the Scots. In the south-west, first Devon and then Cornwall had been absorbed by Wessex.

Between some half a million and one million people lived in England at the beginning of the Viking Age. The population structure was probably comparable to that of a developing country in the modern world. In other words, life expectancy was worse than in England today, but better than during the Industrial Revolution. In the typical Middle to Late Saxon community represented in the cemetery at Raunds (Northamptonshire), the average life expectancy at birth was 21 years. Infant mortality was high; a sixth of all children died before reaching the age of two; a third were dead before they reached their sixth birthday. If one survived to the age of 12 one's chances of a long life were better; the average life span was now 33 years, and a few individuals reached the ripe old age of 60 or more. In fact, 12 seems to have been widely recognised as the age of maturity; the laws of Æthelstan decreed that any man over 12 years old could be killed if found guilty of theft. Poor hygiene and nutrition was probably the most common causes of death. Childbearing females were most at risk; at Raunds men were much more likely to reach their late 30s than women.

Anglo-Saxon society was rigidly hierarchical, and a small aristocracy lived off the labour of a great many peasants. At the top was the king and his *ealdormen*. The Danes and eleventh-century Anglo-Saxons called them jarls or earls. Then there were the *thegns*, or landholders, who later became knights or lords of the manor. Next there were various grades of agricultural workers, and finally a substantial slave class, possibly up to a quarter of the population.

Most of the population lived in the countryside, where the mixed-farming economy would have been familiar to Viking settlers. In the lowland zone of southern and eastern England, towns were already emerging before the Viking Age. London and York acted as centres of royal and ecclesiastical administration, as well as of trade and industry. A special class of trading ports, or *wics*, such as *Hamwic* (Southampton) and Ipswich played an important role in foreign trade. Most people lived and worked in wooden buildings; stone was reserved for churches. The Anglo-Saxons were Christians, erecting stone crosses and burying their dead in Christian graveyards.

Danish Vikings sailing westwards along the north-west coast of Europe would have been funnelled into the English Channel from where they could attack the wealthy south coast of England and the north coast of France. For Norse Vikings sailing directly west across the North Sea, the east

coast of England was their natural landing point. It provided
a number of sheltered inlets and suitable harbours, as well as
unprotected monasteries; river estuaries gave access to the
interior of the country. Many sailed round the north coast
of Scotland to Orkney and the Hebrides and continued
down into the Irish Sea, from which they could raid north-
west England and south-west Scotland, together with Wales,
Ireland and the Isle of Man.

THE CAUSES OF VIKING EXPANSION

Historians have been much exercised in trying to explain
the Viking raids, although some have suggested that they
were simply an extension of normal Dark Age activity made
possible and profitable by special circumstances. Certainly
the Viking expansion westwards would have been impossible without their famous longships. Ships were an essential
means of transport around Scandinavia; in the eighth century
the Scandinavians developed fast, light, easily manoeuvrable
vessels which made long sea journeys possible. Their ships
gave Vikings the advantage of surprise and a means of swift
retreat. Yet whilst the ships may have made the raids possible
they cannot be seen as sufficient cause by themselves.

The descendants of Norse emigrants believed their
ancestors were fleeing from the tyrannical growth of royal
power in Norway. Certainly in the Isle of Man they seemed
to avoid creating any excessive central authority, and may
have been trying to preserve an archaic form of society.
Norway was also undergoing a dramatic growth of population, with massive forest clearances in the east but limited

room for expansion in the west. Bjorn Myhre has played down the extent of dramatic change in Norway around AD 800. He argues that Viking raids in the late eighth and early ninth centuries should be seen as acts of chieftains acquiring wealth and silver, but probably also as part of a conflict between a heathen Germanic culture in the north and Christian kingdoms in the south and west. The beginning of the Viking Age should be defined as the point at which the Danish and Norwegian petty kingdoms were so powerful that their chieftains felt strong enough to begin raiding overseas (Myhre 1993; 1998).

No doubt a number of factors were working in combination, but it is necessary to remember that Viking activity in England lasted, with a break, for some 250 years, during which time Scandinavian society was also undergoing considerable changes. Whereas initial raids in the late eighth and early ninth centuries may have been targeted at the acquisition of portable wealth, which could be fed back into a Scandinavian gift exchange-based economy, later activity was sometimes directed more towards the acquisition of land.

In Denmark, excavations of Viking Age villages have revealed the emergence of magnate farms, or large privately owned estates, in the later ninth and tenth centuries. Whereas land had previously been held by an extended family group or tribe, now it was granted to individuals and passed on to their children. Rune-stone monuments may represent new inheritance claims as much as memorials to the dead. At the top, Gorm and his son Haraldr were unifying Denmark under the rule of a single king. Their power is symbolised by the distribution of Trelleborg forts throughout their kingdom, and by the royal grave at Jelling. The Viking raids may therefore represent increased competition between the elite groups. With estates being passed to eldest sons, and distributed by rulers to their followers, there would be less and less land to go round in Scandinavia. To maintain the system expansion was essential, and the easiest way to expand was overseas, where land, wealth and prestige could all be sought. No doubt the lure of easy treasure was still an incentive and Vikings may have switched between trading, raiding and settling, according to which was the most advantageous strategy. Nonetheless, an underlying trend can be observed. As the basis of status in the Scandinavian world shifted from the possession of portable wealth and the ability to give gifts of silver arm rings, so the purpose of Viking attacks shifted away from the acquisition of silver towards the acquisition of land, initially for the individual, and then later for the state.

2

VIKING RAIDS

Any account of Viking raids has to be derived primarily from historical sources, which for England means the Anglo-Saxon Chronicle. Archaeological evidence is a poor witness to particular events. Political upheavals, such as those which affected York in the mid-tenth century, apparently went wholly unnoticed in Coppergate, where business was much as usual. Nevertheless, remains of fortifications, war cemeteries, memorials and hoards, together with Anglo-Saxon loot found in Scandinavia, all contribute to our knowledge of Viking activity.

Historical sources are more explicit but they may also be less reliable. They were compiled by those on the receiving end of Viking attacks, and suffer from the usual problems of wartime propaganda. In particular, the size of the enemy forces seems to have been widely exaggerated. In ninth-century references to Viking forces in the Anglo-Saxon Chronicle a distinction can be drawn between six small fleets of between three and 23 ships, for which the numbers of ships appear to have been counted exactly, and four larger fleets each estimated in round figures greater than 80. The armada of 350 ships recorded for 851 looks suspiciously like a multiplication of the previous largest number (35) by ten.

It has also been pointed out that to translate the Anglo-Saxon word here used in the Chronicle to refer to Viking raiding forces as 'army' or 'host' may be misleading. In seventh-century laws any group larger than 35 is defined as a *here*. Given that Viking ships are likely to have had crews of some 30 men, or 50-60 at the most, then most Viking raiding parties may have been counted in hundreds, and even the larger forces may still have been under 1000. We do know that in 1142 it took 52 ships to carry a force of less than 400 mounted knights across the Channel (Sawyer 1971).

The Anglo-Saxon Chronicle does allow us to distinguish several phases of Viking activity, stretching over some 250 years. It would undoubtedly be foolish to regard the Viking Age as a single phenomenon. Viking forces surely fluctuated in nature and size as the motives for their campaigns developed.

PHASE 1: SPORADIC RAIDS AND LOOTING, 789-864

From the late eighth century onwards, small groups of Viking raiders were sailing up the English Channel, and round the north of Scotland into the Irish Sea, exploiting possibilities for trade or plunder as they arose.

Some time during the reign of Beorhtric, king of Wessex (786-802), three ships of 'Northmen' (from Horthaland in Norway) landed at Portland on the Dorset coast (see chapter 1). The king's local representative, or reeve (whose name was

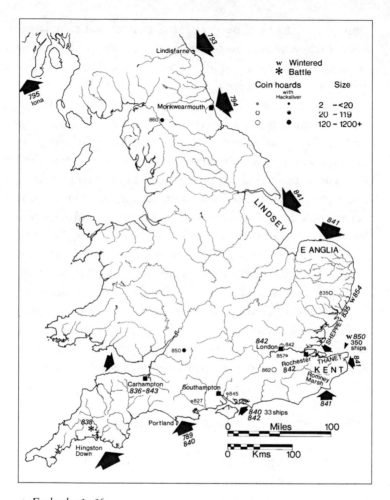

w Wintered
* Battle

Coin hoards
with
Hacksilver

Size

○ •   2 – <20
○ •   20 – 119
○ •   120 – 1200+

793

795
Iona

Lindisfarne

794

Monkwearmouth

860○

841

LINDSEY

841

E ANGLIA

835○

SHEPPEY 835 w 854

842
London ▲ 842

857○

862 ○

Rochester

842

w 850
350
ships

841

THANET

KENT

Romney
Marsh

850 ●

Carhampton
836-843

Southampton

○827

○845

838

Portland

789
840

Hingston
Down

840 33 ships
842

841

0   Miles   100

0   Kms   100

2 England, 789-864

Beaduheard), appears to have assumed that the visitors had come to trade and directed them to a nearby royal estate at Dorchester. Unfortunately the supposed traders turned out to be raiders and killed the reeve with all his men (Keynes 1997). The significance of the event was obvious to the late ninth-century West Saxon chronicler who, even if he associated the raiders with contemporary Danish armies, could see with the benefit of hindsight that 'Those were the first ships of Danish men which came to the land of the English'.

It was the attacks on the Northumbrian monasteries that excited most consternation; in 793 the Anglo-Saxon Chronicle recorded:

> In this year dire portents appeared over Northumbria and sorely frightened the people. They consisted of immense whirlwinds and flashes of lightning, and fiery dragons were seen flying in the air. A great famine immediately followed these signs and a little after in the same year, on 8 June, the ravages of heathen men miserably destroyed God's church on Lindsifarne, with plunder and slaughter.

Alcuin reacted with indignation and horror:

> Lo, it is nearly 350 years that we and our fathers have inhabited this most lovely land, and never before has such a terror appeared in Britain as we have now suffered from a pagan race, nor was it thought that such an inroad from the sea could be made. Behold the church of St Cuthbert spattered with the blood of the priests of God, despoiled of all its ornaments; a place more venerable than all in Britain is given as prey to pagan peoples.

Clearly Alcuin was shocked by what was reported to him although his remarks must be seen as those of an expatriate Archbishop of York now residing in Aachen. We believe that the blood-spattered monks were back looking after their monastery a matter of months later.

The fact that in 792 King Offa was making arrangements for the defence of Kent against 'pagan peoples' suggests that there were other, unrecorded, raids. In 804 the monastery of Lyminge, an exposed site north of Romney Marsh, acquired a refuge within the walls of Canterbury. These early raids should be seen in the context of the Norse colonisation of Shetland, Orkney and the Hebrides. Norwegian raiding groups sporadically targeted English sites, but England was not troubled much until the second quarter of the ninth century, when the Danish attacks commenced. From 835 the Chronicle records a series of heavy raids on the south coast by Danish forces, culminating in 850, when the Danish army wintered in England for the first time:

> In this year Ealdorman Ceorl with the contingent of the men of Devon fought against the heathen army at *Wicganbeorg*, and the English made a great slaughter there and had the victory. And for the first time, heathen men stayed through the winter on Thanet. And the same year [851] 350 ships came into the mouth of the Thames and stormed Canterbury and London and put to flight Brihtwulf, king of the Mercians, with his army, and went south across the Thames into Surrey.

The chronicler's remarks suggest that these events were considered in retrospect to mark the next stage in the escalation of Viking activity in England.

Hoards

In troubled times it was prudent to keep your money buried. Finds of Viking Age hoards may sometimes be related to raiding activities, but care should be exercised in their interpretation. Hoards were normally buried with the intention of recovering them later; they only stayed buried, to be retrieved much later, under special circumstances, such as the death of their owner. Dating their burial can also be problematic. The most recent coin is normally taken to indicate the date of deposition, but savers' hoards may contain mainly old coins.

It appears possible to distinguish between hoards deposited by Vikings and those hidden by the English (Blackburn and Pagan 1986; Kruse 1980). Viking hoards may include coins, ingots, ornaments and other fragments of silver ('hack silver'), which has often been nicked or pecked to test its purity. Silver from the Cuerdale hoard (Lancashire) (*plate 25*) had been nicked from 5 to 20 times on average (Graham-Campbell, ed. 1992). The earliest Viking hoard was found at Croydon (Surrey) in 1862. It appears to date from 872, when the Vikings wintered in London, and probably represents the accumulated loot of a member of the Viking army. The hoard comprised 250 coins, three silver ingots and part of a fourth, and four pieces of hack silver, in a coarse linen bag. The coins included pennies from Wessex, Mercia and East Anglia, and Arabic and Carolingian issues (Brooks and Graham-Campbell 1986). Some Viking hoards might contain no coins at all, such as the 19 silver ingots from Bowes Moor (Durham) (Edwards 1985), the silver neck ring and Irish penannular brooch from Orton Scar (Cumbria), and the silver thistle brooch from Newbiggin Moor, Penrith (Cumbria).

English hoards, by contrast, contain only Anglo-Saxon coins, as foreign issues were excluded from circulation, and the coins do not generally show any evidence of having been tested. England had a full money economy, where coins, despite variations in weight and purity, had an agreed face value. The late ninth-century hoard from Bolton Percy (North Yorkshire), for example, contained 1775 copper stycas buried in a small Badorf ware pot. Several hoards contain personal treasure hidden for safekeeping. Around 875 a wealthy Anglo-Saxon hid his best jewellery and some money in a leather purse in Beeston Tor Cave (Staffordshire). The hoard contained two silver disc brooches and a gold finger ring, as well as a number of plain bronze rings and some 50 Anglo-Saxon silver pennies.

Viking armies

There is no direct archaeological evidence for the great battles which dominate the Anglo-Saxon Chronicle's account of the Viking Age, although it has been claimed that the remains of a Viking army have been discovered at Repton (Derbyshire) (Biddle and Kjølbye-Biddle 1992). The site was first noted in 1726, when Dr Simon Degge recorded in his journal a visit to Repton and the story told to him by a labourer, Thomas Walker, aged 88. About 40 years earlier Walker had been clearing some ground when:

> near the surface he met with an old Stone Wall, when clearing farther he found it to be a square Enclosure of Fifteen Foot . . . In this he found a Stone Coffin, and with Difficulty removing the Cover, saw a Skeleton of a Humane Body Nine Foot long, and round it lay One Hundred Humane Skeletons, with their Feet pointing to the Stone Coffin . . .

Excavation in a mound in the vicarage garden at Repton has since confirmed some aspects of this story (*plate 2*). The mound had been constructed over a massive two-roomed stone structure, originally built in the eighth century, west of the monastery church. It is likely that this was originally intended as a mausoleum for the Mercian royal family. The original building was aligned east-west, and was entered down a slight ramp and through a narrow doorway in the centre of the west wall. An internal doorway directly opposite led into the eastern compartment, which had been reused as a charnel house. In the ninth century a low pebble mound had been constructed over the truncated mausoleum, its edges defined by stone kerbing. This was a substantial structure, some 13 x 11m in diameter, and would have been visible from the river Trent. A burial of four teenagers had been cut into the mound, interpreted by the excavators as sacrificial victims. From the charnel deposit, the disarticulated remains of at least 249 individuals were recovered. In the north-east corner was a stack of sorted long bones which may represent the only surviving part of the original burial; the rest of the bones were in a disorganised heap which post-medieval pottery and clay tobacco pipe fragments suggests had been disturbed in the seventeenth century or later, possibly by Walker. The central burial did not survive, but the deposit contained many objects which may originally have accompanied it, including an axe, two large seaxes, and fragments of silver and silver gilt with cloisonné work, possibly from a sword hilt. There was also a small group of coins deposited some time after 871.

Analysis of the main burial deposit underlines that this was an incomplete skeletal assemblage. Thus although there were 249 left femurs there were only 221 skulls and 201 pelvis bones. Smaller bones were very under-represented, with only 1.5 per cent of phalanges (finger and toe bones) for example. This strongly suggests that the assemblage must have been gathered from elsewhere. Nor was it a normal population: 80 per cent were robust males in the age-range 15-45; there were no children or younger teenagers. Although some of the bones showed signs of injury, these had healed and none had apparently died of their wounds. Radiocarbon dating of the bones may suggest that there were at least two assemblages which had been amalgamated; one belonging to the late ninth century and the time of the over-wintering of the Great Army in 873-4; the other to many years earlier. It has been suggested that the Repton burial deposit represents a war cemetery of remains of the Viking Great Army gathered from various battlefields, intermingled with the disturbed remains of the Mercian royal family. More prosaically the bones may represent the occupants of the monastic cemetery, originally buried around the church, but disturbed and re-buried when the massive ditch was dug through the cemetery for the Viking winter camp (see below).

PHASE 2: PERMANENT COLONISATION, 865-96

From 865 it is possible to detect a change in the nature of Viking activity, with large armies arriving with the aim of permanent settlement in England. They were highly mobile forces, moving rapidly around the country, attacking the weakest Anglo-Saxon kingdoms in turn, and exploiting Civil War in Northumbria. In 871, after a year of battles against the

Danish armies, King Æthelred died, and was succeeded by his brother Ælfred.

During the next decade there were three partitions of land between the Danes and the English, in Yorkshire, East Mercia, and East Anglia:

> And that year [876] Healfdene shared out the lands of the Northumbrians, and they proceeded to plough and to support themselves.

> Then in the harvest season [877] the army went away into Mercia and shared out some of it, and gave some to Ceolwulf.

> In this year [880] the army went from Cirencester into East Anglia, and settled there and shared out the land.

Nevertheless, the settlements did not stop the Vikings plundering the rest of England. In 878 they drove Ælfred into Somerset, where he took refuge in the marshes of Athelney. Regrouping his forces he defeated the Danish leader Guthrum at Eddington, and at the Treaty of Wedmore in 886 a boundary was established between Ælfred's Wessex and Guthrum's East Anglia 'Up the Thames, and then up the Lea, and along the Lea to its source, then in a straight line to Bedford, then up the Ouse to Watling Street'. The area to the north and east of this line was later known as the Danelaw, to distinguish that part of the country where Danish custom prevailed, in contrast to the areas of Anglo-Saxon law. The significance of the treaty, however, was also that Guthrum was subsequently baptised, and incorporated into an Anglo-Saxon system of kingship. Ælfred made use of the treaty to consolidate his

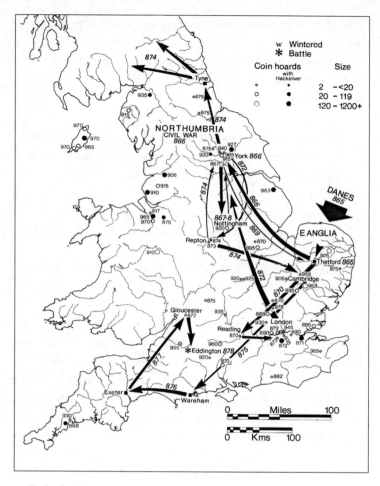

3 *England, 865-96*

position in Wessex. He initiated a system of defended towns, or burhs (see chapter 4), organised a militia system whereby his peasant army was always half at home and half on active service, and built fast and high ships with 60 or more oars 'neither of Frisian design nor of Danish, but as it seemed to himself that they might be most useful' (ASC 897).

From the 890s there were further attacks on Wessex by fresh group of Vikings, but Ælfred's defensive measures proved effective and in 896 the Viking army dispersed. Some settled in East Anglia and Northumbria, others sailed to Normandy. The Chronicle recorded that 'by the grace of God, the army had not on the whole afflicted the English people very greatly'.

The Anglo-Saxon Chronicle does not describe events in the north-west, but an eleventh-century Irish account, supported by references in Welsh sources, records the settlement in the Wirral (Cheshire) of a band of Vikings under the leadership of Ingimundr who had become fugitives after their expulsion from Dublin in 902. This appears to have lead to internecine warfare between Danes and Norwegians, particularly after 919, when the Norse took control of York.

In southern England, Ælfred's policies were continued by his daughter Æthelflaed, who married Æthelred, king of Mercia, and then by his son Edward. Gradually the Danelaw was re-conquered by Ælfred's children. By 917-18 the Danelaw was back under the control of Edward the Elder but this did not lead to the expulsion of the Danes. In fact the Chronicle records that Edward used both Danes and English to man the fortifications at Nottingham in 918, and we hear that both Danes and English submitted to him and swore to keep the peace. Edward's task was made easier by the fact that there were easier pickings for Viking raiders elsewhere in Europe. In 920 the Northumbrians and Scots submitted to Edward, and after the Battle of Brunanburh in 937, Danish power in the north collapsed. In 954 Erik Bloodaxe, the last Viking king of York, was expelled from the city.

Viking fortifications

Viking armies wintering in England needed to camp in a defensible position. At first they appear to have made use of natural islands, such as the Isle of Sheppey and Thanet, but from the late ninth century there are a number of references in the Anglo-Saxon Chronicle to purpose-built fortifications. In 885 the Danes 'made fortifications round themselves' at Rochester, and in 892 they built forts at Milton Regis, near Sittingbourne, and at Appledore, on the edge of marshes between Rye and Ashford, in Kent. In 893 there are references to forts at Benfleet and Shoebury on the Essex coast, and in 894 a fort was built by the River Lea, about 32km (20 miles) above London, and another at Bridgnorth on the River Severn. In 917 they 'made the fortress at Tempsford, and took up quarters in it and built it, and abandoned the other fortress at Huntingdon'.

These forts were probably fairly rudimentary, comprising an earthwork bank-and-ditched enclosure, perhaps with a timber rampart. Such earthworks are notoriously difficult to recognise and to date archaeologically, and one must be cautious of sites with names such as that of Dane's Dyke (Yorkshire) which are likely to be earlier landscape features which were attributed to the Vikings in antiquity. Nevertheless, there are several possibilities, and one excavated example, particularly along the Danelaw frontier. All would have sheltered an army in the hundreds, rather than the thousands.

The Chronicle references suggest that the Vikings preferred to make use of the sea or a river or marsh to protect them on one side, and at these sites one might expect to find a D-shaped enclosure, such as those erected around Scandinavian coastal trading sites such as Hedeby and Birka. The fort at Gannock's Castle, near Tempsford, has often been described as Danish but is now recognised to be a twelfth- or thirteenth-century site. In fact, the fort at Tempsford referred to in the Anglo-Saxon Chronicle is more likely to have been a 2ha (5-6 acre) site adjacent to the river Ivel at Beeston, near Sandy (Bedfordshire), 5km (3 miles) south of Tempsford. Others may be observable in modern town plans, and Nicholas Brooks has suggested that the line of the King's Ditch represents a D-shaped Viking camp at Cambridge.

A number of similar D-shaped sites have been identi-fied in Bedfordshire, at Church Spanel, where a gravel island has been artificially fortified with a bank, at Stonea Camp, where an enclosure was built against the Fen edge, and at Bolnhurst. Willington and Etonbury (Bedfordshire) and Longstock (Hampshire) may be comparable sites with provision for protecting boats within them in dry-docks and harbours (Dyer 1972). At Repton, a D-shaped enclosure was constructed as a winter camp for the Viking army of 873-4. The river Trent formed one side; the rest of the site was surrounded by a bank and ditch into which the monastery church was incorporated as a gatehouse. The ditch, which cut into the Anglo-Saxon cemetery to the east of the church, was a massive affair, some 4m deep and 4m wide. It has been estimated that the Repton fort would have taken five weeks to construct with 200 men. At Shoebury (Essex) a rampart enclosing a semi-circular area, approximately 460m across, adjacent to the sea, may be the Viking camp of 893.

Where a suitable site was not available adjacent to water then circular fortifications may have been constructed, although none as fine as the Danish Trelleborg forts have been found. A number of possibilities have been identified, with wide ditches and internal banks, or regular circular hollows with low banks, although without excavation such sites might equally well be Roman amphitheatres or Norman ringworks. Limited excavation has demonstrated that Warham Camp (Norfolk) originated in the Iron Age, although the site may still have been remodelled in the Viking Age (Gray 1933). At Howbury (Bedfordshire) there is an almost perfectly circular enclosure, 40m in diameter, with ramparts 3m high with a wide water-filled ditch on the outside. The site commands the highest spur east of Bedford, and gives a view along the Ouse Valley. At Hawridge Court, on the Hertfordshire-Buckinghamshire border, there is a regular earthwork with a flat central area, 60m in diameter, with a bank 5m high and a ditch still 1m deep. Finally, at Ringmere (Norfolk) there is another circular enclosure, 32m in diameter, with a double bank and ditch.

Ritual deposits

There is also a large quantity of material, weaponry in particular, which has been discovered in rivers. In 1965 it was calculated that 34 Viking Age swords had been found in English rivers, as opposed to eight from churchyards and Viking graves (Wilson 1965). Twenty-four of these were from the river Thames or its tributaries. Spears, axes, knives and tools have also been found. Eight axes, six spearheads, a pair of tongs and an anchor have been dredged from under Old London Bridge alone (*plate 3*). These finds have often been interpreted as evidence of Viking battle losses, with Viking warriors storming London, for instance, being dumped in the river along with all their armour, weapons and tools. This seems unlikely. A find from Skerne (East Yorkshire) perhaps reveals the true nature of these deposits (Dent 1984). At Skerne a number of animal skeletons and Viking metalwork have been found closely associated with the oak piles of a bridge abutment or jetty. In total there were at least 20 animals, including horses, cattle, sheep and dogs. Only one showed signs of slaughter: a horse had been pole-axed in the forehead; none showed signs of butchery for consumption. Four knives, a spoon-bit, an adze and a Viking sword in a wooden scabbard of willow poplar with fleece lining were also found. There are similar finds from Scandinavia, continuing an Iron Age tradition of bog offerings of horses and weapons, at sites such as Illerup (Denmark). These deposits were probably ritual sacrifices, perhaps offered to give thanks for success in a previous battle, or in the hope of good fortune in a forthcoming one.

PHASE 3: EXTORTION OF TRIBUTE, 980–1012

By the second quarter of the tenth century there was clearly a well-established Anglo-Scandinavian society in the Danelaw, and England enjoyed several decades of peace. Towards the end of the tenth century, however, the new generations of Vikings were no longer able to plunder Russia and turned their attention back to the west. These new armies differed from those of the previous century in that they now included Swedish Vikings (Jansson 1966; 1990) as well as Danes and Norwegians, and in that they apparently had no interest in settlement, but used their power to extort tribute, or Danegeld, from the native population. Edgar of Wessex had been recognised as king of all England, and even the Christianised Danish population had recognised him as their overlord. After Edgar's death in 975 there was a period of dynastic weakness. His son Edward was murdered in Corfe Castle, and Æthelred (the Unready), succeeded to the throne. From 980 onwards the Anglo-Saxon Chronicle records renewed raiding against England. At first the raids were probing ventures by small numbers of ships' crews, but soon grew in size and effect, until the only way of dealing with the Vikings appeared to be to pay protection money to buy them off:

And in that year [991] it was determined that tribute should first be paid to the Danish men because of the great terror they were causing along the coast. The first payment was 10,000 pounds.

Over the next decade payments grew dramatically, causing widespread hostility to the Vikings, and leading to demands for increasingly desperate reprisals. On St Brice's Day (13 November) 1002 Æthelred 'ordered to be slain all the Danish men who were in England'. The intended victims of this drastic measure can hardly have been established Danish settlers in the Danelaw, and it was probably directed against remaining groups of mercenaries, or paid-off members of the army who had outstayed their welcome. Nonetheless, amongst those slaughtered were the sister and brother-in-law of Sveinn, King of Denmark.

The English lacked any consistent policy and effective means of defence against the Viking threat, and the later compilers of the Anglo-Saxon Chronicle become increasingly scathing about Æthelred:

> and when [the Danes] were in the east [in 1010], the English army was kept in the west, and when they were in the south, our army was in the north. Then all the councillors were summoned to the king, and it was then to be decided how this country should be defended. But even if anything was then decided, it did not last even a month. Finally there was no leader who would collect any army, but each fled as best he could, and in the end no shire would even help the next.
>
> All these disasters [in 1011] befell us through bad policy, in that they were never offered tribute in time nor fought against; but when they had done most to our injury, peace and truce were made with them; and for all this truce and tribute they journeyed none the less in bands everywhere, and harried our wretched people, and plundered and killed them.

The Viking warbands were probably mounted and highly mobile. Stirrups are thought to have been introduced by the Vikings. Many Danish graves contain stirrups and other rich horse equipment. Finds of stirrups in the Danelaw attest to the presence of Danish cavalry in eleventh-century armies (Graham-Campbell 1992; Seaby and Woodfield 1980).

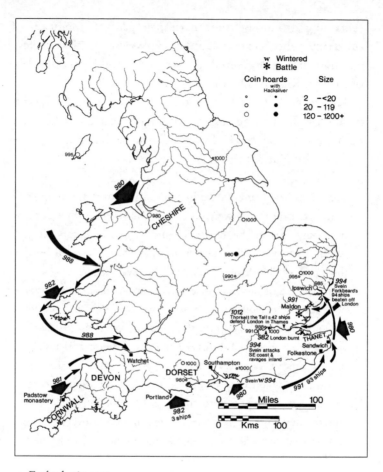

w Wintered
✳ Battle

Coin hoards
with
Hacksilver   Size

·   ·   2 – <20
o   •   20 – 119
○   ●   120 – 1200+

995 ○

○ 1000

980
CHESHIRE
○ 980

○ 1000

988

982

980 ●

990 ○

995 ○   ○ 1000

Ipswich

991
Maldon

1012
Thorkell the Tall's 42 ships
defend London in Thames

988 ○   ○ 1000
991 ○

982 London burnt

994
Svein attacks
SE coast &
ravages inland

985

994
Svein
Forkbeard's
94 ships
beaten off
London

980

THANET

Sandwich

Folkestone

988

Watchet ■

○ 1000
DORSET

Southampton
○ 1000
980 ○

Svein W 994

991 93 ships

981
DEVON

Padstow
monastery ■

CORNWALL ✝

Portland ■

982
3 ships

980

0   Miles   100

0   Kms   100

4 *England, 980-1012*

Scandinavian evidence

A few Anglo-Saxon objects found in Scandinavian graves testify to the looting of English monastic sites. They include mounts, such as the gilt copper alloy plaques stripped from book covers and placed in ninth-century Norwegian female graves at Bjørke and Alstad, shrines, and a silver hanging bowl found at Lejre, Sjælland (Denmark). There are also a number of Anglo-Saxon style swords from Denmark, and an Anglo-Saxon gold ring found in a ninth-century context at Hon, Haug (Norway) (Bakka 1963).

Generally, however, finds of ninth-century Anglo-Saxon coins are comparatively rare in Scandinavia, and there are only 125 English and Frankish coins of the ninth century, distributed between some 50 finds (many of which are probably later deposits anyway), compared with some 4000 Arabic coins. There are several possible explanations. English coins may have been melted down, or perhaps conditions in Denmark allowed the hoarders to collect their treasure. Alternatively the ninth-century raiders may have settled rather than returned to Scandinavia, and used their loot as capital with which to settle.

Whilst there is little evidence in ninth- and early tenth-century Denmark for raiding, by the later tenth and eleventh centuries there is much more evidence for contact with Anglo-Saxon artefacts and artistic influence. From 990-1040 more Anglo-Saxon coins are found in Scandinavian hoards than are known from the whole of England, demonstrating the significance of the Danegeld payments. They include c.50,000 Anglo-Saxon pennies from Gotland, c.2600-3000 from Norway, and c.15,000 in some 115 hoards from the area controlled by Denmark. English coins are also found as far

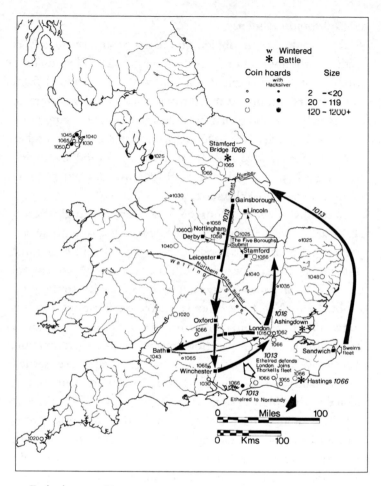

5 *England, 1013-1066*

afield as Finland, Russia, Poland, the Baltic Republics and Germany. These hoards contain little hacksilver, indicating that the raiders were being bought off in coin. Sometimes they appear to represent the modest profits of a common warrior, such as the 34 Æthelred pennies buried beside a large stone in Vestermarie on Bornholm; sometimes they are larger, such as the 600 coins placed in a cowhorn and buried on the beach at List on the island of Sylt. The payment of Danegeld had to be underwritten by a huge balance of payments surplus; this could only be achieved by stimulating exports and cutting imports, itself accomplished through currency devaluation.

PHASE 4: POLITICAL CONQUEST, 1013-66

In the early eleventh century, Viking activity in England entered a final phase. In 1013 Sveinn of Denmark arrived with a Viking army, not for the extortion of tribute, but for the conquest of the kingdom. The Chronicle recorded that 'all the nation regarded him as full king' and Æthelred fled to Normandy. The next year, however, Sveinn died, and Æthelred was able to return, but in 1016 a new Viking force arrived under Sveinn's son Knutr. At the Battle of Ashingdon Knutr was victorious, and at the subsequent treaty of Olney it was decreed that he should succeed to Mercia and the Danelaw, whilst Æthelred's eldest son, Edmund Ironside, should have Wessex. Edmund, however, died shortly after, leaving Knutr as king of England, Denmark, Norway and 'part of the Swedes too'. Knutr's kingdom, based at Winchester, reached far beyond the bounds of the old

Danelaw. Knutr ruled as a Christian monarch, founded a number of churches, and went on pilgrimage to Rome. The scale of his empire, and the nature of his kingship, are a measure of how far the Viking warrior had become a medieval ruler. On Knutr's death in 1035 Denmark and England became separate kingdoms again, and remained so, apart from a brief interval from 1040-2 when the English invited Hartacnut, Knutr's son and successor in Denmark, to be their king. By the time the last great Viking leader, Harald Hardrada, was killed at Stamford Bridge and William of Normandy, descendant of Viking settlers in Normandy, beat Harold at Hastings, the Viking Age in England was really over, although Viking influence carried on.

3

VIKING COLONISATION

Both the impact and the scale of Viking colonisation have
been much debated. The traditional view is of a mass
migration which overturned existing political, social, and
economic organisation, but few scholars now accept that
whole regions were overwhelmed; the process is now
seen as geographically variable, much more gradual, and
involving far more assimilation of native traditions (Hadley
1997). Scandinavian settlers were not pioneers carving farmsteads out of a virgin landscape. The England they found
was already intensively farmed, with few open expanses
where newcomers could establish their own villages. Nor
was the settlement a free-for-all, with individuals seizing
land as they chose. Land was allocated by Viking leaders in
reward for military service, and they would expect to receive
tribute irrespective of whether the land was held by their
followers or by Anglo-Saxons. For many peasant farmers the
Scandinavian settlement probably just meant a change in
whom they paid their taxes to.

SETTLEMENT PATTERNS AND GREAT ESTATES

Before the Viking Age most rural land in England was organised in large estates, sometimes called 'multiple' estates, because they typically grouped together several component areas, each with complementary resources, under common ownership (Hadley 1996; Jones 1965; Unwin 1988). These estates are well known in Celtic regions such as Wales, where they have tended to survive longer, but they have also been mapped in Cumbria, Northumbria, and the East Midlands. Their antiquity is uncertain, but they probably developed out of the areas over which petty lords were owed payments of food and services, possibly going back to post-Roman times. These lords also sought to divide up extensive upland grazing and hunting areas and place them under the control of their estate centres in the adjacent lowland arable areas. The great estates in the Kentish lowlands, for example, included woodland in the Weald, and may also have had coastal rights for fishing and salt production. In Middle Saxon England these estates were in the hands of kings, major lordly families, and the Church. The monastery at Lindisfarne, for example, owned extensive tracts of northern England, which would be leased out to farmers, or run by estate managers. Land was rarely owned by individuals, however, being vested in communities or families. Individuals only had a life interest and could not make grants which would, in effect, disinherit their heirs.

From the ninth century onwards, however, there were fundamental changes in land ownership which led to the fragmentation of the great estates over much of lowland England and the rise of the private landholder. These changes might still have taken place without Viking intervention, as

Anglo-Saxon kings made permanent grants of land to their followers in order to secure their loyalty. Nevertheless, they were undoubtedly hastened by the Scandinavian settlement, and also provided a mechanism for it. Scandinavian colonisation brought about a massive privatisation of land ownership. Viking leaders gained land by conquest and also by purchase, disrupting traditional landholding patterns.

In some cases Viking settlers simply took over existing estate centres, using the established administrative structure to gain control of all the estate. In the north-west, for instance, many of the major territorial divisions bear names of Scandinavian origin, such as 'copeland' which means 'bought land' in Old Norse. In many cases, however, Viking leaders divided estates amongst their followers in reward for military service. The large number of parishes in the Danelaw, particularly in Lincolnshire and the East Riding of Yorkshire, may reflect Healfdene sharing out the lands of the Northumbrians in 876. The few large parishes which were retained, such as those of Pickering and Beverley, may be those estates which remained under royal or episcopal control.

In 914, following the Battle of Corbridge, Ragnald seized the lands of the Lindisfarne monks, giving some to his followers, Scula and Onlafbal. In the tenth century, charters record the sale of land by Scandinavians in Bedfordshire, Derbyshire, and probably Lancashire. At the beginning of the eleventh century, in a classic protection-racket gambit, Æthelred was forced to grant land in Oxfordshire to a Dane called Toti in return for a pound of gold needed in order to pay Danegeld.

The Domesday Book records the end result of this process of fragmentation, with much of England under the control of large numbers of individual manors. In some areas, frequently those with less evidence for Scandinavian settlement, such as the Kentish Weald, the large estates survived, although Scandinavian settlers were not the only new landholders. There are records, for example, of English lords buying land within the Danelaw. Nevertheless, it was the Scandinavian settlement which paved the way for the buying and selling of small parcels of land in the tenth century.

As a complementary process we might expect to see changes in settlement patterning, with the foundation of local manors and the development of villages and parishes around them. Certainly, over much of England there does appear to have been a shift away from a large number of dispersed settlements to the nucleated villages which are recorded in the Domesday Book. Evidence collected so far however suggests that the precise date of this change varies between different parts of country, and there is nothing to link it directly to the Scandinavian settlement. Indeed, in some areas it has been suggested that the Scandinavian contribution may have been to delay the process of nucleation, and led to the retention of the pattern of dispersed settlement preferred in Norway. In Cumbria, for example, a combination of cultural and geographical factors meant that the parish system never completely evolved into the small-sized units typical elsewhere. Cumbria retained a dispersed pattern of small hamlets and individual family farms, rather than the nucleated villages of south and central England. Even in the south the fragmentation of holdings was irregular by the time of the Domesday Book, the size of parishes being influenced by the resources available within a given region.

LOCAL GOVERNMENT AND LAND ADMINISTRATION

Whilst Viking colonisation may have had a major effect on settlement ownership and organisation, there is little firm evidence that it led to fundamental changes in the administrative system of England.

The major administrative unit was the county. The boundaries of the English shire counties, as they remained up until the 1974 local government reorganisation, were drawn up in the tenth and eleventh centuries. In the East Midlands they took their names from the *burh* towns, of Derby, Nottingham, Leicester and so on, and the county may have been that area which was attached to the *burh* for its defence (see chapter 4). The size of Lincolnshire and Yorkshire may therefore have been a defensive measure against renewed Viking attacks.

Within each shire the basic unit of local government was the 'hundred' or 'wapentake'. 'Hundreds' are first mentioned explicitly in a document of Edgar's reign (959-75); their name was originally based on a taxation unit of 100 hides, each hide being a unit of land required to support one family. Each hundred had its estate centre, or *vill*, to which the estates' inhabitants paid their rents and services. Each hundred also had an open air meeting place, where land transactions took place, cases of theft or violence were heard, and some local policing functions were organised. Secklow (Buckingham-shire) is one of thirteen meeting places which have been excavated in England (Adkins and Petchey 1984; Reynolds 1999). It was found to consist of a mound, 25m in diameter, surrounded by a roughly circular ditch, some 1m deep, constructed in the tenth century. Such meeting places were often positioned near landmarks, such as at crossroads, on a parish boundary, or near a prehistoric feature, such as a standing stone.

In the Anglo-Saxon area the hundreds survived as administrative districts into the post-conquest period and are recorded in the Domesday Book. In Northamptonshire, for example, there were some 28 hundreds. In North and West Yorkshire, on the other hand, the local administrative divisions are described as 'wapentakes', although there is no simple correlation between wapentakes and Scandinavian settlement as hundreds were preserved in the East Riding of Yorkshire. In any case the process of government was probably the same, as 'wapentake' is derived from the Old Norse *vapnatak*, which refers to the flourishing of weapons in consent at an assembly.

In the multiple estate system, the central area to which outlying settlements were attached is often described by the term 'soke'; the 'sokeland' comprised those settlements which owed tribute and services to the lord. Such references were once thought to refer only to Viking leaders taking over Anglo-Saxon estates within the Danelaw and settling their followers around them. 'Sokemen' mentioned in the Domesday Book were thought to represent those free peasants who were descended from Viking settlers. In fact, the paucity of sokemen in Yorkshire has suggested to others that this is unlikely to be true, and sokes are believed to be of great antiquity; sokemen are now seen to be just as likely to be English peasants as Vikings.

The use of the 'ploughland' as a unit of assessment for taxation purposes has also been seen as a Scandinavian introduction, but since there is no evidence for its use in

Scandinavia until the thirteenth century, and since the 'hide' continues in use in the Danelaw, it is just as likely to represent an eleventh-century fiscal system. Similarly, the duodecimal numbering system of counting in dozens and half-dozens has been seen as a Scandinavian introduction with assessments in multiples of 5 and 10 in the south and west, and more often in multiples of 6 and 12 in the Danelaw. Yet the evidence is far from clear cut, and in Normandy it is the decimal system which is seen as being Scandinavian in origin.

PLACE-NAME EVIDENCE

Each age leaves traces of its settlement pattern in the names given to places and, although the first recorded mention of most place-names is in the Domesday Book, with care it may be possible to identify those 'Scandinavian' names given during the Viking Age.

In general, the distribution map of Scandinavian place-names confirms the evidence provided by the written sources (*6*). Hardly any Scandinavian names, for example, are found south of the Danelaw and the recorded settlements in Yorkshire, Mercia, East Anglia and the Wirral can all be seen to have left their mark. Nevertheless, there are some areas where place-names modify the picture provided by the written evidence. There are some Scandinavian names outside the Danelaw in Northamptonshire and Warwickshire, for example, and a concentration in the Lake District, for which there is no documentary evidence.

Within the Danelaw there is considerable variation in the density of Scandinavian names. Kenneth Cameron (1958;

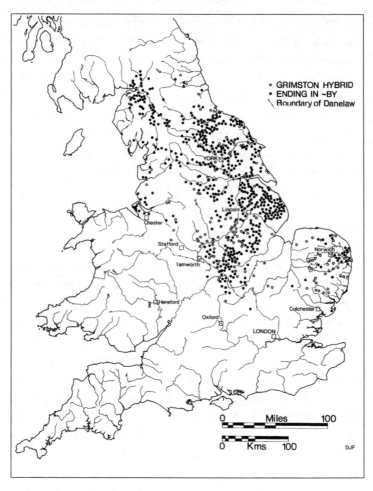

6 Map of Scandinavian Grimston hybrid and -by place-names (after Hill 1981 and Roesdahl et al. 1981)

1965; 1970; 1971) and Gillian Fellows-Jensen (1968; 1972; 1975; 1978; 1985) have each compiled comprehensive regional surveys of Scandinavian place names. They have found, for example, that there are few Scandinavian names in the north-east (Durham and Northumberland) and in Cambridgeshire and the south-east (Essex and Hertfordshire). In the East Midlands, Scandinavian influence is most marked in Lincolnshire, Nottinghamshire and Leicestershire. In Cheshire, Scandinavian names are concentrated in the Wirral (Gelling 1992). Within Yorkshire, a grand total of 744 Scandinavian-influenced place-names are recorded in the Domesday Book, although Scandinavian influence is less marked in what was the West Riding. In the East Riding 48 per cent of names are of Scandinavian influence; in the North Riding 46 per cent; and in the West Riding 31 per cent.

The type of name may help to identify the origin of the settlers, although care must be exercised as Danish words such as -*thorp* may have been adopted by Norse settlers. Nevertheless, Normanby, for example, probably denotes a Norwegian settlement. Norwegian names predominate in the north-west, where a 20km (*c.*12-mile) belt along the Lancashire coast seems to have been reclaimed from sea marshes by Norwegian farmers, possibly expelled from Ireland. English names only appear on the higher ground further to the east, and in east Cheshire and Staffordshire a sprinkling of Danish names may mark the western limit of the Danish conquest of Mercia. In the north-west, Celtic names are also sometimes compounded with Norse ones, such as Aspatria (Patrick's ash).

There are four main categories of 'Scandinavian' place-names. Firstly, there are some 850 *by*-names, such as Aislaby,

Balby, Brandsby, Dalby, Ferriby, Kirby and Selby, containing
the Old Danish word *by*, meaning a farmstead or village. The
English equivalent was to use the ending *-ton*, as in Beeston,
but the new word passed into English and is used in the term
'by-law' to mean the law of the village. We can compare, for
example, the place-names Osmondiston and Aismunderby,
representing Osmund's *tun* and Asmund's *by* respectively.
There are some 220 *-by* names in Lincolnshire, and some
210 in Yorkshire. In Lincolnshire they are concentrated in
the Wolds and have been interpreted as farmsteads of immigrants who had sailed up the Humber estuary. In Yorkshire
they are concentrated in the Vale of York. In Derbyshire,
Leicestershire, and Nottinghamshire there are a further 85
-by names, with 22 in Northamptonshire, 21 in Norfolk,
and 3 in Suffolk. Many of the *-by* names are compounded
with a Scandinavian personal name. In Yorkshire, of the 119
-by names which comprise a personal element 109 (over 90
per cent) are Scandinavian, 7 are Old English, and 3 are Old
Irish.

The second place-name ending which has been interpreted as indicating a Scandinavian settlement is *-thorp*, as
in Bishopthorpe, Danthorpe, Fridaythorpe, Newthorpe, and
Towthorpe. The Old Danish word *-thorp* is generally taken to
indicate some form of secondary settlement, and these sites
have been seen as representing subsequent exploitation of
marginal land, or as outlying dependencies of estates which
had their centres elsewhere, and that may have been detached
from those centres by the Vikings. In Yorkshire there are some
155 place-names ending in *-thorp* recorded in the Domesday
Book, and 109 in Derbyshire, Nottinghamshire, Lincolnshire
and Leicestershire. The *-thorp* names are less frequently linked

with a Scandinavian personal names, and have therefore been regarded as being later than the *-by* names.

Thirdly, there is a class of place-names known as 'Grimston hybrids' which combine a Scandinavian and an English element, such as a Scandinavian personal name with the English *-ton* in Burneston, Catton, Saxton, Scampston, Wiggington, as well as Grimston itself, or *-hide*, as in Olaveshide. In Lincolnshire and Yorkshire there are some 55 Grimston hybrids; in Derbyshire, Leicestershire and Nottinghamshire some 50. These names are often thought to represent English villages that were acquired by Scandinavian settlers, but perhaps remained outside direct Scandinavian control.

Finally, changes in the pronunciation of Anglo-Saxon place-names, to avoid un-Scandinavian sounds, have also been taken as evidence for Scandinavian settlement. Thus the Anglo-Saxon Shipton becomes Skipton, and Cheswick becomes Keswick.

The high proportion of these four classes of Scandinavian style place-names recorded in the Domesday Book has been used as one of the main arguments in support of a substantial Scandinavian colonisation of England. It is argued that even if it is accepted that the Anglo-Saxon Chronicle's account of the size of Viking armies is exaggerated, there must have been a substantial secondary migration of colonists in order to account for the large number of Scandinavian place-names.

However, there are two difficulties with this argument. The first problem is a linguistic one. We cannot be certain that individual Scandinavian place-names were coined by Viking Age settlers. Few place-names are recorded before the Domesday Book of 1086, some 200 years after the

Scandinavian settlement, and as distant from them as we are from Napoleon. In the intervening years the English may have adopted many Scandinavian words into common usage, and may have adopted Scandinavian naming habits themselves. We do know that Scandinavian names were being coined as late as the twelfth century. Given that it is now accepted that there were Scandinavian elements in the fourth- and fifth-century Anglo-Saxon invaders, it might also be possible that some Scandinavian names may have been adopted earlier. Even if we could be sure that the Scandinavian names belong to the Viking Age, rather than earlier or later, we still cannot be certain that they were coined by Scandinavians. Indeed, the people responsible for naming a settlement will not usually be those living in it, but those from neighbouring sites who need to refer to it, or tax it. Thus the name Ingleby might suggest a village of the Angles, named by Danes.

The second problem concerns the age of those settlements that received Scandinavian names. If they are evidence for a massive Scandinavian migration then they should be new sites on virgin ground, but many may simply have been new names for existing places, just old estates under new management. Excavation at Whitby and Osbournby, for example, has revealed evidence for pre-Scandinavian settlement at both these sites. It is now widely accepted that much of England was already intensively farmed at the beginning of the Viking Age. If so, then the high proportion of Scandinavian place-names must represent a renaming of existing settlements.

Many Scandinavian style place-names involve the endings *-by*, *-thorp* or *-ton* compounded with a personal name. In Yorkshire and the East Midlands 40-60 per cent of names ending in -*by* have a personal name as their first element. This can be explained by the fact that it was during the Scandinavian settlement that much land passed into small-scale private ownership. Previously land had been held in the great or 'multiple' estates, frequently under group ownership. In the Viking Age these large estates were broken up and their component elements were handed out to individuals. Scandinavian place-names, therefore, mark not so much an extension of settlement as its reorganisation under new lords. Their density reflects not so much the areas of migration as areas of break-up of older great estates into individual ownership. The Yorkshire Wolds, for example, was a very fertile area which had been farmed intensively from the late Iron Age. The large number of settlements bearing Scandinavian names are not new sites, but dependencies of estates based around the Wolds which were taken over by Scandinavians. We can therefore see which estates were preserved and which were broken up. The area around Bardney Abbey, for example, has no Scandinavian place-names, in contrast to the area around Whitby where there are many.

There is no need to postulate, therefore, a mass folk migration in order to explain the distribution of Scandinavian place-names. Names are given to places when it becomes necessary to refer to them unambiguously. The Anglo-Saxon Chronicle records three partitions of land between the Scandinavians and the Anglo-Saxons, in Northumbria, Mercia, and East Anglia (see chapter 2). In each case the Viking leaders rewarded their followers with alloca-tions of land. Both the new farmers and those expecting tribute from them would have been keen to legitimise their claims to this land, and what better way than by naming it after them? As the habit of buying and selling land developed in the tenth century it remained important to identify the owners, be they Anglo-Saxons or Scandinavians.

LINGUISTIC CHANGES

It is often suggested that other linguistic evidence provides clear proof that the Scandinavian settlements were on the scale of mass folk migrations. Scandinavian pronouns, verbs and other everyday words, such as the words for husband, knife and window, were adopted by the English language. Some have contested that such changes could not have occurred unless the Vikings were in a majority, but other linguists have persuasively argued that it is misleading to draw conclusions about numbers on the basis of linguistic changes (see Ekwall 1930; Hines 1991; Page 1971; Townend 2000). They suggest that the influence of one language upon another depends on their relative status, and by the need to borrow words to describe new things. It is unlikely that ninth-century Northumbrians would have been able to understand Danes and Norwegians easily. Communication would rely on a few individuals who knew both languages. Nevertheless, the similarity between Danish and English would mean that it was easy for the English to adopt Scandinavian words. In particular, the introduction of a large number of Scandinavian words associated with farming indicates that there was an influential Danish-speaking farming population. Most evidence suggests that Scandinavians adopted English fairly rapidly, adding a few of their own words. Vernacular inscriptions from north and east England show a clear continuity in the use of English from the eighth to the eleventh centuries. There is no evidence for Scandinavians continuing to use either their runic script or their own language in England.

PERSONAL NAMES

The number of individuals bearing Scandinavian personal names has also been used as a measure of the density of Scandinavian settlement (Fellows-Jensen 1968; Insley 1994). The number of Scandinavian personal names compounded with settlement names in Yorkshire and Lincolnshire has already been noted. In the Domesday Book 40 per cent of names in Derbyshire are Scandinavian; as are 50 per cent in Nottinghamshire and in Cheshire. Of course, name-giving habits change with fashion, and are particularly prone to influence from the elite, as testified by the number of children named after royalty, media stars or footballers. Scandinavian names may have increased in popularity during the Viking Age, but they do not necessarily denote Scandinavians. Members of the same family mentioned in Domesday have both Scandinavian and Anglo-Saxon names. It also tends to be forgotten that written sources are restricted to the elite group. Most of those individuals mentioned in the Domesday Book are referred to as manor holders. Name-giving may reveal more about class allegiance than ethnic identity (Hadley 1997).

Coins record the names of the moneyers who were responsible for coin production (Smart 1986). The proportion of Scandinavian names increases from zero under Ælfred to 3 per cent under Edward the Elder, 5 per cent under Æthelstan, to 15 per cent under Eadred and his successors. Regionally there is considerable variation. In York *c*.75 per cent of names are Scandinavian by the reign of Æthelred; in Lincoln *c*.50 per cent, Chester *c*.25 per cent, and London *c*.7 per cent. Yet even if all these individuals were born in Scandinavia they hardly represent a cross-section of tenth-century England. Name-giving habits may well have been profoundly affected by the Scandinavian settlement, but Scandinavian names may still have been confined to the land-owning and mercantile classes.

In summary, settlement organisation and language cannot be used as evidence for a substantial Scandinavian migration. What place-names do show is that whatever the size of the invasion, its political implications should not be underesti-mated. A major consequence of the Viking raids was the frag-mentation of the great estates. The Vikings stimulated a new market in the buying and selling of property. Land was taken into private ownership, and often named for the first time.

ARCHAEOLOGICAL EVIDENCE

Few Viking Age rural settlements have been excavated, and even fewer can be positively identified as the homes of Scandinavian settlers (7). The first problem is that most of the successful farmsteads must have grown into medieval villages, and now lie buried under their modern successors. The second is that the typical rural excavation yields few finds, making cultural identification difficult. The Anglo-Saxon

7 Map of excavated Viking Age settlements

migrations can be recognised archaeologically from new settlements and building types which appear over southern and eastern England. Yet we cannot assume that new peoples will inevitably introduce new forms of settlement and, particularly if their way of life was identical to that of the existing population, there is no reason why their farms should be distinguishable from those of the indigenous population. Incoming and native peoples may also interact to create new or hybrid forms. Therefore, all the settlement evidence for the period should be considered, ranging from palaces and manorial centres to isolated upland farmsteads.

Our picture of ninth- to eleventh-century royal accommodation is derived from excavations at Cheddar (Somerset). The site probably functioned as a royal estate centre from the second half of the ninth century, and may well have been used by Ælfred. The first phase included a long hall, possibly of two storeys, erected within a palisaded enclosure with a possible gatehouse. The remaining buildings probably served as private residential buildings and offices. Circa 930 the hall was replaced by a more substantial timber hall and a stone chapel. A massive post-hole outside the entrance may indicate that a flagstaff or decorated pillar stood there. The hall was rebuilt a third time in the late tenth century and a raised dais was added, probably during the reign of Æthelred. The relative cleanliness of the site and the lack of spectacular finds suggests that it may only have been occupied periodically during royal visitations, and was stripped to a skeleton caretaker staff in the interim. Documentary sources suggest that the Anglo-Saxon court or *witan* met here three times during the tenth century, in 941 under Edmund, 956 under Eadwig, and in 968 under Edgar (Rahtz 1979 but see Blair 1996).

At North Elmham (Norfolk) excavations have revealed details of life within an episcopal palace complex. A Middle Saxon cathedral community abandoned the site in the early ninth century, possibly as a result of Viking raids, but sometime after 917 the site was cleared and levelled for a new minster and ancillary buildings. A new church was erected over the earlier ruins and a large timber hall, possibly for the use of the bishop, was erected nearby. In the eleventh century a new palace was built elsewhere, and the site was given over to secular use. It was colonised by farmers, with peasant dwellings, sheds and animal pens set in fenced enclosures (Wade-Martins 1980).

Other excavations have illuminated the decline of the great estates and the evolution of the manor during the Viking Age. The extensive landscape project at Raunds has demonstrated the fragmentation of a multiple estate into several component manors over several centuries. At Furnells Manor a Middle Saxon settlement in a ditched enclosure was replaced by a large timber hall, the proto-manor house, in the early tenth century. A small stone church was built adjacent to the enclosure. At about the same time, the first regular tenements of peasant farmers were being laid out at Furnells and West Cotton, marked by ditched enclosures. As none of the ditches could have offered more than minimal protection their main purpose must have been for laying out. Indeed, the evidence at West Cotton shows that equal plots, c.20m wide, were created (Cadman and Foard 1984; Foard and Pearson 1985).

A similar process may have been taking place in another area of Scandinavian settlement, at Wharram Percy (North Yorkshire). The South Manor site at Wharram was occupied from the early eighth century. The date of the laying out of the peasant tofts and crofts is still uncertain, but probably took place during the Viking Age, in the tenth century (Hurst 1984; Beresford and Hurst 1990). The lack of Late Saxon pottery from the fields between the villages, compared with the abundance of Middle Saxon sherds, suggests that the villages in this area were also becoming nucleated at that time. Significantly there was continuity of the elite site from the Anglo-Saxon to the Anglo-Scandinavian phase at Wharram. In the seventh and eighth centuries there was a post-built hall and an associated weapon smithy on the site that was to become the South Manor after the Norman Conquest. This hall was replaced, and the new residence has not been found, but the weapon smithy continued in operation somewhere in the vicinity, and a sword hilt guard has been excavated, similar in appearance to one from Coppergate. There were also honestones of a type of stone peculiar to Norway, and a strap end and belt slide decorated in the Borre style, current in Scandinavia in the ninth and tenth centuries (Stamper and Croft 2000). If not Norwegian himself then the new tenant of Wharram Percy had certainly adopted Scandinavian dress fashions.

In some cases a mother settlement might be replaced by a number of daughter sites. At Chalton (Hampshire), for example, the Church Down site was abandoned by the ninth century, but the nearby villages of Chalton (Manor Farm), Idsworth and probably Blendworth were occupied from about this time. At Cottam (East Yorkshire) parts of an eighth- and tenth-century landscape have been examined as a result of collaboration between archaeologists and metal detectorists (Richards 1999). The first settlement comprised a number of post-built halls set in an enclosure and adjacent to an ancient trackway. This site was rich in metal artefacts and I have suggested that it may have been a local centre for a Northumbrian royal vill at Driffield. In the late ninth-century, however, this site was abandoned. A weathered skull, a possible execution victim, was dumped in a pit adjacent to one of the buildings, and sealed with rubbish, including a coin of AD 858-64. The settlement now shifted to an adjacent site approximately 100m to the north, where an Anglo-Scandinavian farmstead was constructed. The new farmstead comprised a number of regular planned sub-rectangular enclosures (*plate 4*). It had been badly damaged by later ploughing but there were clusters of post-holes representing a number of buildings, at the head of a ditched trackway. The entrance to the site was a very grand affair, comprising a massive external ditch, an internal rubble bank, itself possibly topped by a timber palisade, and a timber gate superstructure. Given the lack of ditches around the rest of the site this must have been constructed for status rather than defence. Associated tenth-century finds include a Borre-style buckle, a Jellinge-style brooch, and a pair of so-called Norse bells (*plate 32*) (see chapter 7). This need not necessarily mean that the inhabitants of the tenth-century farmstead were Scandinavian settlers who had dispossessed their Anglian predecessors. Nonetheless the ostentatious new farm suggests *nouveau-riche* farmers, or old farmers identifying with a new elite. Occupation of the new site was short-lived, however. During the tenth century the settlement shifted again, and new sites laid out which developed into the deserted medieval villages represented by earthworks of tofts and crofts at Cottam and Cowlam.

Many pre-Conquest manorial residences were set within fortified enclosures. In some cases existing fortifications were utilised. At Portchester (Hampshire), several substantial timber houses were erected within the walls of the former Roman fort in the late eighth or ninth centuries. Finds of east Mediterranean glass and coins of Burgred of Mercia testify to the relative wealth of the site. In 904 it was acquired by the king as a royal *burh*, but it never became a town and appears to have continued to function as a manor site. In the late tenth century a substantial aisled hall and three subsidiary buildings were constructed, served by impressive timber-lined wells. Massive dumps of food waste may represent the remains of great feasts. In the early eleventh century the owner erected a free-standing flint and masonry tower, some 6m square, on a plot of land between the hall and the subsidiary domestic buildings. This may have been a bell-tower or chapel, as it became a focus for burials. It brings to mind that one of the requirements of an eleventh-century *thegn* was that his property should have a bell-tower (Cunliffe 1976).

At Faccombe Netherton (Hants) an aristocratic residence has been excavated on the north-east edge of Salisbury Plain. It may be that which was mentioned in a will of *c*.950 as belonging to a noblewoman named Wynflæd, who was probably the mother-in-law of King Edmund. The residence comprised an aisled hall, a building of private apartments with a latrine, and a separate kitchen. In the early eleventh century the site was redesigned with a substantial bank and ditch. By this stage a church had been built adjoining the manorial complex (Fairbrother 1990).

Another late tenth- to early eleventh-century *thegn*ly residence has been excavated at Sulgrave (Northamptonshire). The parish church, which is Anglo-Saxon in origin, is on the same alignment as a tenth-century timber hall and may have originated as a private chapel. At Sulgrave a separate stone building set to one side of the timber hall may have been the base of a separate belltower. The residences at Sulgrave, and at Goltho (Lincolnshire) were each surrounded by a defensive ditch (Davison 1968).

At Goltho an early ninth-century farmstead was superseded by a fortified earthwork enclosure, in which a fine bow-sided hall like that at Cheddar, a bower, a kitchen, and weaving sheds formed three sides of a rectangular enclosure. The kitchen would have provided food for feasts when followers were entertained in the hall. The fortifications comprised a 6m-wide rampart topped by a timber palisade, surrounded by a ditch 5.4m wide and 2-2.4m deep. They are as substantial as those protecting the *burhs* at Cricklade and Tamworth, and must have been constructed for serious defence, perhaps against the threat of Viking raids. The manorial complex may have been founded by a member of the Saxon aristocracy, although the discovery of a Scandinavian-style bridle bit could be used to argue that it was a late ninth- or tenth-century Viking foundation. During the late tenth and early eleventh centuries the site underwent considerable expansion. The hall was replaced by an aisled version without internal partitions, which would be more suitable for use on official occasions and for estate functions, and the bower was enlarged and partitioned, with a latrine attached to it at one end. After the Norman Conquest it developed into a motte-and-bailey castle (Beresford 1987).

Not all rural sites developed into manorial complexes. Catholme (Staffordshire) was already in decline before the

Viking Age and was abandoned in the early tenth century.
During its latest phase the settlement comprised groups of
buildings linked by fences, defining paddocks or small yards.
Within the central enclosure a bow-sided hall was the most
substantial building (Losco-Bradley and Wheeler 1984).
Tenth- and eleventh-century buildings set within ditched
or fenced enclosures have also been identified at St Neots
and Little Paxton (Cambridgeshire) (Addyman 1969; 1972).
These appear to represent individual farm units with ancillary
buildings, wells, homefields, and droveways leading to a village
centre. Other sites, whilst not large enough to be described as
villages, comprise more than single farmsteads. At Springfield
(Essex) nearly a dozen rectangular houses of the ninth to
eleventh centuries have been excavated. The suggestion of a
rectangular tower may mark this as another proto-manorial
site; although the 15 rubbish pits contained few rich finds
there was evidence for pottery and quernstones imported
from Germany (Buckley and Hedges 1987).

Other settlements developed into what might be called
small towns, at least by the Norman Conquest. At Steyning
(West Sussex) there was an extensive agricultural settlement
and market. The settlement must already have been important
by 858 when Ælfred's father Æthelwulf was buried in the
minster church. Continental imports reached the town by
river, with Pingsdorf and Beauvais ware vessels. Excavations
have revealed a large part of an enclosed settlement dated to
the tenth and eleventh centuries, with a gateway and two
post-built halls. It appears that across the whole site buildings
were loosely scattered in a number of similar enclosures,
representing a number of independent farm units, but with
no evidence of formal planning. By Domesday there were

123 substantial houses but although the occupants were labelled as town dwellers their lives would have been indistinguishable from those of a rural farmer (Gardiner 1993; Gardiner and Greatorex 1997).

Within the upland zone of the north and west of England there was a vigorous upturn in the rural economy during the Viking Age (see chapter 6). In Cumbria there was a major settlement expansion into the under-utilised wastelands of the central Lakeland massif and other marginal areas. This is unlikely to have been common ground which could be easily colonised. On a multiple estate even the most barren land would still have been put to some use, and would have belonged to someone, even if it was not inhabited. Nevertheless there was apparently a considerable Scandinavian takeover in the tenth century, probably following the historically recorded expulsion of the Hiberno-Norse Vikings from Ireland in 902. Nine out of ten place-names in the central Lake District show Scandinavian influence, although Gaelic elements suggest that settlers from the Hebrides, Faroes and Iceland, as well as Dublin and Man may also have been involved. Cumbria was exposed to seaborne attack along a considerable coastline and the topography made defence difficult. It has been suggested that the Anglo-Saxon aristocracies survived, but were deprived of much of their land and were now in competition with the colonists. There was an immigrant hierarchy of mixed British, Gaelic or Scandinavian extraction at the apex of society, with little sign that it was distinctively Viking.

In Northumbria the place-names associated with the upland clearances are as much Anglo-Saxon as Scandinavian. In some areas of Durham and Cleveland, it has been suggested that significant numbers of Danish immigrants filled the crucial middle and lower ranks of land ownership, and were able to consolidate their position by exercising patronage in favour of their fellow countrymen. By the early tenth century, however, all the evidence suggests a community moving towards cultural and ethnic integration.

Extensive survey work within the uplands has led to the identification of increasing numbers of abandoned farms, but such sites are notoriously difficult to date, and even when excavated rarely yield any material which allows us to say that they are the farmsteads of Viking settlers. One such settlement has been excavated at Ribblehead (North Yorkshire), set on bare limestone pavement at an altitude of 340m above sea level (*8*). The farmstead comprised three buildings set in an enclosed farmyard with an associated field system of over 1.2ha (3 acres). The main building was a longhouse; the others comprised a bakery with a grindstone and limestone oven and a poorly built smithy with a central sandstone slab for a hearth, and remains of iron scale and cinders. The few artefacts recovered suggested a mixture of agricultural and simple craft activities. They included an iron cow bell, a horse bit, a spear head, two iron knives and a stone spindlewhorl. Local materials were used for most needs and the site was largely self-sufficient, although four Northumbrian stycas found within the wall suggest small-scale monetary transactions, and date the construction of the site to some time after the late ninth century (King 1978).

A similar range of artefacts has been recovered at Bryant's Gill (Cumbria) where a farmstead has been located at the centre of a 20ha (50 acre) field system at 290m above sea level, in the north-west fells of Kentmere (Dickinson 1985).

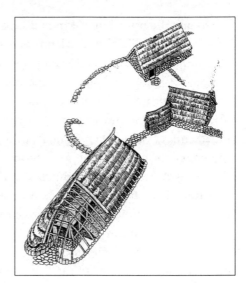

8 An artist's reconstruction of Ribblehead. A flagged pathway leads from the main house to the kitchen. The third building was probably a workshop. Courtesy Yorkshire Museum

The finds from in and around the longhouse included charcoal and iron slag, stone spindlewhorls and over 20 honestones (*plate 10*).

At Simy Folds (Durham) three sites have been examined. Each consists of the stone foundations of a single long narrow building with one or two subrectangular buildings at right angles to it, arranged to enclose a yard. The site lies within an extensive field system of prehistoric origin. The pollen evidence suggests that cereals were being cultivated during the Viking Age, as well as the keeping of livestock, including sheep, cattle and pigs. The finds once more include a stone spindlewhorl and honestone and a quernstone. The quantities of iron slag suggest that iron-working was being undertaken on a large scale, presumably based on the local iron ore (Coggins *et al.* 1983).

Despite the notorious Viking raid it appears that the island of Lindisfarne (Northumberland) was occupied throughout the ninth century. At Green Shiel a large farmstead comprising a group of buildings linked by enclosing walls and yards has been investigated adjacent to the beach (O'Sullivan and Young 1995). The site was first noticed in the middle of the nineteenth century when stone from the walls was robbed in the course of constructing a waggonway from lime kilns in the dunes. At least three longhouses and a number of ancillary structures have been identified (*plate 29*). Although there is no clear association with the monastery, the large quantities of cattle bones mean it is possible that this was a lay farm supplying vellum to the monastic scriptorium. Two ninth-century Northumbrian stycas were found during the nineteenth-century work; subsequently a further 16 copper alloy stycas and a silver penny of Æthelred of Wessex (866-71) have been recovered during the excavation. The finds also include an Anglo-Saxon spear-head, a large iron key, a fragment of bone comb and an amber bead.

Similar ninth- and tenth-century farmsteads have also been recognised in the south-west, at Gwithian, Tresmorn and Treworld (Cornwall) and at Hound Tor and Hutholes (Devon). The latter sites may have been the equivalent of Norse shielings, occupied by herdsmen who grazed their stock on the open moorland pastures during the summer months (Beresford 1971; 1979; Dudley and Minter 1966).

At Mawgan Porth (Cornwall) excavations have revealed a coastal hamlet of three or more farmsteads with groups of long-houses and ancillary buildings terraced into the hillside, and its own cemetery set uphill and to the west. Each farmstead may have represented a single extended family.

The most completely excavated farmstead consisted of four major buildings set around a central courtyard. The largest building could have housed some four or five people. The settlement was probably occupied from the mid-ninth to the mid-eleventh centuries, but this settlement form continued in use into the Middle Ages. The inhabitants were pastoralists, shellfish gatherers and fishermen. They had virtually no iron tools and used stone, bone and pottery extensively. A coin of Æthelred II, *c*.990-5, shows that they maintained some contact with Wessex (Bruce-Mitford 1997).

In summary, there is little evidence for a mass peasant migration of new settlers, clearing land. Rather, a Scandinavian elite presided over the fragmentation of great estates, establishing manorial centres and accelerating the market in the buying and selling of land. Many settlements were named during the Viking Age, and concentrations of place-names indicate the adoption of Scandinavian terms into local speech in many areas. Taken together with the great variety of Scandinavian personal names in use by the eleventh century they indicate communities maintaining aspects of a Scandinavian identity in some parts of the Danelaw. Archaeology cannot help us to discover Viking farmsteads, but it does reveal new settlement forms associated with people using artefacts, as well as language, to proclaim an Anglo-Scandinavian ethnicity.

4

THE GROWTH OF TOWNS

The Viking Age witnessed an explosion in the development of towns (Clarke and Ambrosiani 1991). At the start of the period there may have been less than a dozen places, all trading sites, which we would regard as urban centres. By 1066 there were more than 100 places with some claim to be regarded as towns (9). Nevertheless, they still contained only a fraction of the population, perhaps some 10 per cent. They included a great diversity of forms, from those that were little more than fortified royal estate centres such as Stafford, to massive cosmopolitan emporia such as York. Nonetheless, most had a Domesday population of more than 1000, with the larger towns such as Lincoln and Norwich with over 5,000 townsfolk.

How far was the growth of trading and market sites a result of Viking stimulus, and how far was the development of fortified towns a reaction to the Viking threat? Did the Scandinavian settlers establish any towns of their own? Would towns have developed anyway, if there had been no Scandinavian influence? Was there anything particularly Scandinavian about the character of the towns or their defences? Excavations within many English towns and cities over the last three decades mean that we are now closer to answering these questions.

WICS

In Middle Saxon England most trade was conducted at large *wics* or camps, such as *Hamwic* (Southampton) and *Eoforwic* (York), on the south and east coasts. These sites apparently developed under royal patronage, so that the traders could be protected, and controlled, and taxes levied. At *Hamwic* there is evidence for a 45ha (110-acre) site of *c.*700-850, sheltering a population of at most 2000-3000 people, enclosed by a bank and ditch (probably to define the trading zone as much as for defence), with properties laid out on a regular street system. A number of sites have been excavated within the Saxon town. At the Six Dials some 68 houses and workshops, 21 wells and 500 pits have been recorded (Andrews 1997). A major north-south road about 14m wide which was regularly resurfaced was constructed first, followed by the digging of the boundary ditch 3m wide and 1.5m deep, before the houses and properties were laid out. *Hamwic* had trading contacts with northern France and the Rhineland; many of its inhabitants made their living from processing imports and exports, and by manufacturing goods from imported raw materials (Morton 1992).

Settlement at *Gippeswic* (Ipswich) began in the early seventh century with an adjacent cemetery, waterfront and

9 *Map of Viking Age towns*

pottery industry to the north-east. This expanded rapidly in the early ninth century to cover an area of about 50ha (125 acres) on both sides of the river Gipping. Metalled roads were established, one which ran over the former cemetery, with buildings set out along the street frontage. Imports of Frankish pottery demonstrate the trading links (Atkin 1985; Scull 1997; Wade 1988).

In London trade was actually transacted on the waterfront, probably from boats pulled up on the shore. Initially there was no need for storage or warehouse facilities, and trading sites may have left few archaeological traces. The location of such markets along the Thames is indicated by *wic* place-names, such as Chiswick, Greenwich, Woolwich and Twickenham.

Some trading sites may have been no more than periodic beach markets, such as Meols, near the mouth of the Dee Estuary. The name is derived from the Old Norse word for sandbank, *melr*, and it has been suggested that a pre-Viking beach market may have been taken over by Norse traders. Finds include some 20 Anglo-Saxon pennies of the late tenth and eleventh centuries, and a variety of metalwork, including Hiberno-Norse-style copper alloy ringed pins, and a mount with Scandinavian-style animal ornament (Bu'lock 1960).

At most *wic* sites, however, the threat of attack in the Viking Age led the traders to seek protection within walled towns, and may also have disrupted trade. At almost every site occupation declines or ceases during the ninth century. At *Hamwic* it has been argued that the coin finds indicate that it was already in decline before the Viking raids, although others have concluded that it was increased Viking activity which disrupted its trading networks. The site appears to have been gradually depopulated from *c.*850; there was occasional pit-digging up to 900, but no new buildings can be identified (Morton 1992; Andrews 1997).

At Fishergate, York, where an area of Anglo-Saxon Eoforwic has been excavated, a single coin of the 860s is the latest find, compared with some 40 of the eighth and early ninth centuries; the site was then abandoned until the eleventh or twelfth centuries.

In London, the extensive Saxon settlement of *Lundenwic* was located in the Strand area. The coin finds from this area are mainly eighth- and early ninth-century; the latest are a hoard of *c.*840 from the Middle Temple and a second of *c.*870 from the Thames, found during repairs to the south side of Waterloo Bridge. Both hoards have been linked with documented Viking raids on London. The latest pottery from the Strand area has been dated to the ninth century. By the late ninth century there is little evidence for trade, and virtually no imported pottery. A hoard of Northumbrian stycas found in the defensive ditch around *Lundenwic* suggests that the ditch had been filled in by 867, implying that the *wic* had been abandoned.

At *Hamwic*, *Eoforwic* and *Lundenwic*, the Viking raids seem to have disrupted trade but protection was sought within a defended area, and new sites were established after some delay. In Southampton, *c.*900, the focus of occupation shifted to higher more defensible ground some 0.5km to the south-west of *Hamwic* where it was possible to control both sides of the estuary. Ditches outlined an area of Viking Age occupation with regularly laid out streets within the medieval walled town. The new site had different trading contacts, and a reduced role in long distance international trade;

tenth-century pottery from Normandy is one of the few
identifiable Viking age imports. It has also been suggested
that a short-lived fortified *burh* was established on the site of
the Roman town of *Clausentum*, upriver of *Hamwic*, but it
was probably the important urban centre at Winchester that
inherited many of the functions of *Hamwic* (Andrews 1997).

In London, occupation within the walled area of the
Roman city does not appear to start before the late ninth
century, perhaps reflecting its re-establishment as a fortified
burh by Ælfred in 886 (*10*). The names used to refer to
London also show a change from *Lundenwic* in the early ninth
century to *Lundenburh* in the later ninth century, with a short
period of overlap in the 850s. All coin finds are now from the
City area, indicating that the exposed Strand site between
the river Fleet and Westminster was abandoned, and the old

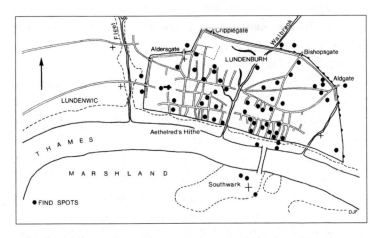

*10 Plan of Viking Age London (after Vince 1990). The majority of the
archaeological finds marked on this map are potsherds of the late ninth to early
eleventh centuries*

Roman fortress was reoccupied. There is little evidence for tenth-century occupation outside the City walls. The Roman walls must still have survived as foundations at least; the ditch may have been recut, and the gates reused. A pit-free zone either side of the wall may indicate the position of a rampart. The Anglo-Saxon Chronicle records that London success-fully held out against the Vikings in the 990s.

Fragments of over 40 buildings have been excavated within the walled city. A regular street plan determined by the position of the Roman gates was established, with gravelled surfaces. Timber halls were erected along the street frontages, and set back from the street, mostly along the back and sides of properties, there were sunken workshops and storage buildings (see chapter 5). Along the tenement bound-aries there were numerous latrine pits, some over a metre in diameter and several metres deep. Layers of cess alternate with tips of garden soil, domestic refuse and floor sweepings. By the eleventh century such pits were often provided with plank and wattle linings, suggesting that their contents were regularly cleared out.

Ælfred's policy of urban renewal is illustrated by grants of plots of land adjoining the trading shore in Queenhithe to the bishop of Worcester and archbishop of Canterbury, along with the exclusive right to moor ships. In effect Ælfred was establishing a partnership with trusted clerics whereby they were responsible for running the port, in return for a share in the profits (Steedman *et al.* 1992). Nonetheless, London only began to prosper again as a port in the late tenth century, with the erection of wharves of clay, timber and rubble against which vessels could be moored. Access to boats would have been by means of cobbled or planked walkways laid out over the embankment down onto the foreshore, as seen at the Thames Exchange site, or by jetties represented by pile clusters, as seen at Billingsgate. London's international trade was only revived in the eleventh century, but then expanded rapidly; by 1050 there was probably an almost continuous artificial bank running in front of the wall in the eastern half of the city. By the mid-eleventh century there was a considerable settlement within the walled city and further settlements in Southwark and Whitehall, although there may still have been some areas which were unoccupied (Milne 1989; Milne and Goodburn 1990; Vince 1990).

A similar picture is emerging from York (Hall 1988; Moulden and Tweddle 1986; Radley 1971). By the eleventh century York was described as a populous city to which merchants came from all quarters, especially from the Danish people (*plate 27*). In the ninth century, however, there is evidence for a hiatus in trade after the decline of *Eoforwic*. The exposed trading site, beyond the confluence of the rivers Ouse and Foss, appears to have been abandoned in favour of a more easily defended area between the two rivers and closer to the Roman legionary fortress (*11*). The walls of the Roman fort survived sufficiently for York to withstand attack in the ninth century. Although breached in several places, much of the fortress wall stood more than 3m high, and the insertion of the so-called Anglian tower into a gap in the walls, at some date before the Viking Age refurbishment of the ramparts, has been taken as evidence for continued maintenance of the defences. Around 900, York's Viking rulers apparently renovated the defences so as to enclose an area bounded by the Roman walls to the north and west and the rivers Ouse and Foss to the south and east, thereby enclosing the riverside

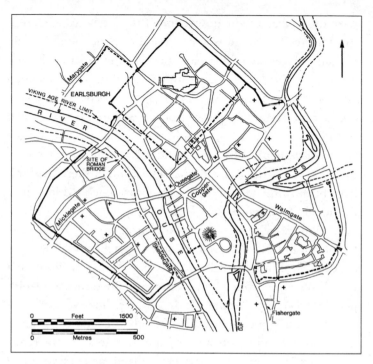

11 Plan of Viking Age York (after Hall 1988)

area to the east of the Roman fortress. An earthen bank surmounted by a palisade was constructed along the north-east and north-west sides of the fortress, and was probably extended down to the rivers, in the same manner as Viking Age defences at Chester (*plate 28*) and elsewhere. There may also have been a defended bridgehead east of the river Foss; although no trace of a Viking Age defensive line has been found beneath the medieval city walls in the Walmgate area, there was occupation and industrial activity in this area. Even excluding this settlement east of the Foss, the total enclosed area of Viking York was some 36ha (87 acres), making it larger than the major Scandinavian towns at Hedeby and Birka.

Within the walled area, however, there is little evidence for Viking Age structures inside the legionary fortress, and in most areas thirteenth-century levels immediately overlie Late Roman ones, although this could be because conditions here were not right for the preservation of Viking Age organic deposits, or because they were swept away *c.*1200 prior to the major medieval building programme. Scandinavian chance finds have been found throughout the area, including manufacturing debris. There is no evidence for the imposition of a regular street layout during the Viking Age, although the Roman defences continued to influence the topography. It has been suggested that the Viking royal palace may have been sited near the south-east gate of the legionary fortress, in King's Square, although no archaeological traces have been excavated. Similarly, no trace was found of the Viking Age Cathedral underneath York Minster although a graveyard with Anglo-Scandinavian grave markers suggests that the church was nearby, possibly to the south-west. The former legionary barrack blocks housed Viking Age activity, including antler and bone working and ferrous and non-ferrous metalworking, with the walls of the former barracks used to demarcate the new tenements. This activity may have been under the control of the church, or may simply have been taking place adjacent to it. In the area between the Roman fortress and Marygate, where there was a defended Roman enclosure, the name *Earlsburgh* suggests that the later pre-conquest Anglo-Scandinavian earls must have had their residence nearby. Between 1030-55 Earl Siward built or rebuilt a church or private chapel here, which he dedicated to St Olaf.

South-west of the river Ouse the area of the former Roman colonia, or civilian settlement, was also occupied during the Viking Age. There is no archaeological evidence for the defences south-west of the Ouse but it is assumed that they were on the line of the surviving medieval walls. There appears to have been an important Anglo-Saxon ecclesiastical complex in the Bishophill area, and the street names point to continued Viking Age activity over most of the walled area. A new bridge was built across the Ouse, to the east of the Roman one, and Micklegate (literally 'Great Street') diverges from its Roman course as it heads for the new crossing. Timber buildings and rubbish pits have been found along Micklegate and on Skeldergate. This new Viking thorough-fare across the Ouse focussed on the Coppergate, Ousegate and Pavement area where the most striking evidence for Viking Age York has been found within the new enclosure. In this area the city has risen on its own refuse, and rich evidence for its people and their lifestyle has been preserved in several metres of Viking Age deposits.

Evidence for intensive occupation, including timber buildings housing leather workers, has been excavated within the basement of Lloyd's Bank, Pavement, and cellared buildings, once thought to be plank-lined tanning pits, have been excavated at High Ousegate, but the largest sample of Viking York has been excavated at Coppergate, on sharply sloping ground leading down to the river Foss.

Post-Roman activity, including glass-working, commences in the mid-ninth century, but it is not clear whether it starts before the Viking takeover as a result of people seeking the protection of the walled town, or as a consequence of the Viking takeover in 866 or settlement in 876. If the

walled town did not include this area until after its Viking
refurbishment then the latter explanation may be more
likely. The new timber Ouse bridge was presumably erected
in the late ninth or early tenth century, and at some time
between the late ninth century and *c*.930-5 the Coppergate
street was established, with a series of long narrow
tenements defined by wattle fence alignments running
back from the street down towards the Foss. These property
boundaries remained in force throughout the Viking Age
and influenced all subsequent developments over the next
thousand years. The plots were of equal width, perhaps
implying that they stemmed from a deliberate act of town
planning designed to stimulate the development of a Viking
Age industrial estate.

On the four tenements within the Coppergate excavations, post-and-wattle buildings were erected on the street
frontage with their gable ends facing the street (*plate 5*). Their
backyard areas were riddled with pits; those lined with barrels
were probably wells; those with wattle lining may have been
used for storage; others served as latrines and cesspits. Within
the buildings there is evidence that iron working and other
crafts were carried out on a commercial scale. Two of the
tenements were used for metalworking, including copper and
lead alloys, silver and gold, as well as iron. In fact, the tremendous diversity of craft activities suggests that the buildings
were rented out to craftsmen, rather than each being perma-
nently occupied by one individual.

Around 975 the four buildings were simultaneously
demolished and replaced by a series of plank-built sunken
buildings (*plate 7*). On three tenements the buildings were
arranged in two ranks, suggesting that the reorganisation was

perhaps prompted by the increased intensity of occupation and the need to store manufactured and traded goods. The buildings were occupied by jewellers and woodworkers, but industrial metalworking ceased and may have been forced to move to the fringes of the densely settled area. Finally, early in the eleventh century, a large warehouse or boat shed was erected at the rear of the site, closer to the river.

The general picture which has emerged from the Coppergate excavations is of a fairly squalid urban environment, which contrasts with that of Roman York. The town has been described as a large compost heap, composed of rotting wooden buildings with earth floors covered by decaying vegetation, surrounded by streets and yards filled by pits and middens with organic waste. Organic refuse was being dumped at a greater rate than it was being cleared away; during the tenth century the ground level rose by an average of 25mm per year. Nevertheless, whilst no doubt the exterior of the properties was foul and disgusting, their insides may have been tolerably cleanly maintained (Hall *et al.* 1983). Excavations of three contemporary late tenth-century tenements from Saddler Street, Durham, have suggested a relatively clean environment, with dumps of sand used to seal middens and pits.

The deposits from Durham are very similar to those from York, although there is nothing particularly Scandinavian about them. Indeed, one must also question whether there is anything distinctively Viking about York, apart from a new taste for Scandinavian style ornament. Certainly, there is no evidence to show that the inhabitants of Coppergate were Scandinavian in origin. As has been shown, Scandinavian traders were not responsible for establishing York and other towns as major trading sites. On the contrary, the international contacts of existing sites were disrupted, and only recovered after an interval. Where there were no existing trading sites, such as on the Isle of Man and in Wales and Brittany, Viking activity did not lead to their formation.

MERCIAN *BURHS*

Although the first Anglo-Saxon towns may have originated as trading sites, a much larger group of towns were established as defended forts, or *burhs*, probably as a direct response to the Viking threat. The earliest English examples were established in Mercia *c.*780–90 by King Offa, possibly following Carolingian prototypes (Haslam 1987). The Mercian *burhs* should be seen as a systematic defence against Viking seaborne attack. All were associated with defensive bridges and were placed on main rivers throughout Mercia so that the *burh* and bridge blocked access upstream to warships. They also functioned as civil and ecclesiastical administrative centres and became important markets, although the markets may have grown up outside the walls without deliberate planning. There appear to have been two classes of site. Some were established on existing fortified Roman sites, where the walls and bridge probably survived; others developed from fortified manorial centres. The Vikings often chose them as military bases in the late ninth century, but the sites were already fortified by this date. A single spinal street normally links the *burh*, bridge and market areas, although the Mercian burhs may have lacked the regular planned street systems which have been observed in the *burhs* of Wessex. Initially, the interiors may have remained fairly open, with intensive occupation only dating from the later tenth century. For their defence they would have relied upon a peasant militia derived from the countryside rather than from within the town (Rahtz 1977).

Traces of early defences at Hereford, and perhaps Tamworth, demonstrate the role of Mercia in the evolution of the Anglo-Saxon town. The town of Hereford commands a strategic crossing point on the river Wye; its name means literally 'the ford of the army'. The town lies on the north bank of the river, where a gravel and clay rampart of the mid-ninth century appears to have enclosed a rectangular area of 13.6ha (33 acres), incorporating the minster church in its south-east quarter. In the early tenth century, possibly at the instigation of Queen Æthelflaed in 914, the walls were extended eastwards to enclose suburban growth across a 21ha (50 acre) area, and improved with timber revetments at front and rear. Finally, *c.*930, the front timber facing was replaced by a stone wall, 2m thick and 2m high, with a slighter wall at the rear, and a fighting platform 4m wide.

The Anglo-Saxon Chronicle records that in 913 Æthelflaed 'went with all the Mercians to Tamworth and built the borough there in the early summer'. This has been identified as a 20ha (50 acre) site of similar plan to Hereford, with a V-shaped ditch and a rampart of turf and stone, separated from the ditch by a wide berm. There is also evidence for a metalled intervallum road behind the rampart, and a bridge to carry the rampart walk over the gateway. As at Hereford, there are archaeological traces of an earlier defence of slighter construction, although this might just be the boundary of a Mercian royal palace, as there is nothing to link it to the burh street system (Gould 1967; 1968).

It is claimed that Stafford was also fortified in 913, although excavations have failed to reveal the *burh* defences. In fact, Stafford has been described as a thinly disguised expansion of a rural manor. In the tenth century there was no regular street grid, and no evidence for planned tenements. The central enclave appears to have contained only the minster church and three centralised crafts: butchery, bread-making and pottery manufacture. The *burh* may have functioned as a collecting station for the agricultural wealth of the neigh-bourhood. Stafford ware pottery was exported to other Mercian centres, but there was no evidence of any other commerce.

Gloucester may also have been founded as a Mercian *burh*, although it is not listed as such. From the sixth to the ninth centuries the shell of the Roman town sheltered a much-reduced population, probably working a number of rural holdings both within and outside the walls. The rapid build up of deposits in the old forum area in the ninth century suggests that animals were stabled here. The people of Gloucester used no pottery, and wooden and leather containers were ubiquitous. They imported little from elsewhere, and the settlement at this stage should probably be seen as a series of small estates, rather than an urban development. In 877 the remnants of the Danish army were able to camp within the town. In the tenth century, however, Gloucester suddenly acquires an administrative and military status. A substantial Saxon timber palace was built on the site of the Roman cemetery at Kingsholm, and the Mercian Council assembled here in 896. At about the same time St Oswald's Minster was founded, and in 914 the inhabitants of Gloucester fended off a Viking attack. Aspects of the street plan may demonstrate an element of planning, with a possible tenth-century surface in the intra-mural St Aldate Street. The Roman walls were refurbished on the east, south and along part of north, but apparently not to the west, where the city had crossed the Roman boundary and extended down to river (Heighway 1984; 1987).

A similar picture of tenth-century revival is emerging from Chester (*plate 28*). The Anglo-Saxon Chronicle records that in 894 ' . . . [the Danes] marched without a halt by day and night, until they arrived at a deserted Roman site in Wirral, called Chester. The [English] levies were unable to overtake them before they got inside the fort, but they besieged it some two days.' The Roman defences must have been largely intact if they could withstand a siege, and in 907 the north and east walls were refurbished with timber by Æthelflaed, and probably extended to the river Dee. An intra-mural gravel road was probably laid at the same time. Within the Roman fortress there were substantial upstanding Roman remains, which were re-utilised as the scale of occupation increased in the tenth century. At Princess Street a sunken building was built within the ruined walls of a Roman barrack block. At Abbey Green Roman buildings were stripped of reusable materials in the tenth and eleventh centuries and new buildings erected alongside. Tenth-century Chester became home to a multi-ethnic trading community, including a substantial Hiberno-Norse element, living to the south of the old legionary fortress, by the river Dee. At Lower Bridge Street at least five cellared buildings were erected in the tenth century and the area surfaced with sandstone chippings. Under Æthelstan, Chester became the most prolific mint in

England; 24 moneyers worked in the town between 924-39. Ironically, it was probably the Irish Sea Vikings who were the main source of the city's prosperity at this time. Finds indicate a wide range of trading contacts, with jewellery in Irish, Viking, and Anglo-Saxon styles. Chester's importance continued until it suffered a Viking raid in 980, and the city itself may have been sacked (Austin 1996-7; Ward 1994).

THE *BURHS* OF WESSEX

In Wessex the Vikings also provided a major stimulus to the development of towns. It is thought that Ælfred, as a means of defence against Viking raiding parties, established a network of *burhs*, such that no part of his kingdom was more than 32km (20 miles) from a *burh*. When Edward the Elder reconquered England from 911-19 he extended the network and fortified a number of new sites (Biddle 1976; Biddle and Hill 1971; Haslam 1984; Hill 1978; Radford 1970; 1978; Williams 1984).

The burghal hidage, a document of c.914-18, lists those *burhs* defending the coasts and frontiers of Wessex, south of the Thames, in the later years of the reign of Edward the Elder. It catalogues 30 *burhs* within Wessex, and a further three outside the kingdom. London is omitted as it was technically part of Mercia; Kent is also excluded. The burghal hidage gives a tax assessment for each *burh*, based upon the extent of its perimeter defences. There are two groups: those generally with a large hidage which were planned as permanent settlements and market centres; their streets still display traces of the original planned layout; and a second class of temporary forts which were comparatively small (less than 16 acres) and were not regularly planned. Only the first category became towns; the second group generally no longer existed by Domesday, and were probably dismantled during the reign of Æthelstan. Most of the burghal forts withered after performing their defensive role although their market function was often transferred to another site, such as from Eashing to Guildford.

Outside Wessex mention should also be made of several Viking Age towns in Kent which were not included in the burghal hidage, but appear to have performed similar functions to the Wessex *burhs*. These include the Roman walled towns at Canterbury and Rochester, and the *wics* at Sandwich and Fordwich, as well as the sea ports at Dover, Romney and Hythe (Tatton-Brown 1988).

Where Iron Age or Roman fortifications survived, *burhs* were often established within the earlier defences. At Pilton and Halwell Iron Age earthworks were probably refortified; at Cadbury the hillfort was reoccupied. In Bath, Chichester, Exeter, Portchester, Southampton and Winchester the *burhs* made use of surviving Roman stone walls and gates. At Bath and Winchester there is evidence that the outer ditch may have been recut during the Viking Age.

Natural defences were also utilised. A large number of *burhs* were established on promontory or peninsular sites, frequently controlling access from the sea. These sites include Axbridge, Langport, Lyng and Watchet in Somerset, *Bredy* (probably Bridport), Shaftesbury, and Twynham (or Christ-church) in Dorset, Burpham and Eashing (Surrey), Malmesbury and Wilton (Wiltshire), Lewes (East Sussex), Lydford (Devon) and *Eorpeburnan* (probably Newenden) in Kent.

1 *The Lindisfarne Stone, Northumberland. A late ninth- or tenth-century grave marker, with a Doomsday scene of a procession of warriors waving swords and axes. The Viking raids on England were often seen as a Judgement; this Doomsday metaphor may have been chosen deliberately.* Courtesy English Heritage

2 *Repton (Derbyshire). The mass grave of 873-4 within the remains of a pre-Viking building.* Reproduced by courtesy of Martin and Birthe Kjølbye-Biddle

3 Viking battle-axes and spears from the River Thames. Courtesy Museum of London

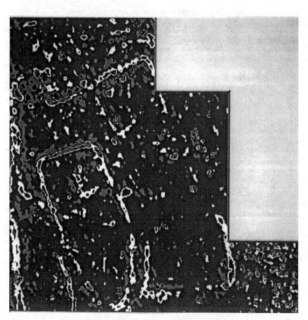

4 Anglo-Scandinavian farmstead enclosures, as revealed by geophysical survey, Cottam (East Yorkshire). Field Archaeology Specialists

5 Four adjacent tenements, Coppergate, York. During the late tenth century there were a series of plank-walled sunken buildings along the street frontage, of which two can clearly be seen. The brick-lined well shaft is a much later intrusion. Courtesy York Archaeological Trust

6 Post-and-wattle wall, Coppergate, York. Courtesy York Archaeological Trust

7 Planked wall of a tenth-century sunken building, Coppergate, York. Courtesy York Archaeological Trust

8 *Wooden cups, bowls and waste turning cores from a woodturner's workshop, York.* Courtesy York Archaeological Trust

9 *The Coppergate grave slab. This stone may well have been intended to form part of a grave memorial at the nearby church of St Mary's. It was found on the Coppergate excavation in a limestone rubble surface. The carving shows no sign of weathering and various details appear to be unfinished, suggesting that it was rejected before completion. Stylistic details suggest that it was produced by the same workshop as the cross shaft from Newgate, York.* Courtesy York Archaeological Trust

10 *Polished stone spindle-whorls and hone-stones, Bryant's Gill, Cumbria. (Board and Trustees of the National Museums and Galleries on Merseyside).* Courtesy of SEARCH Archaeology Group

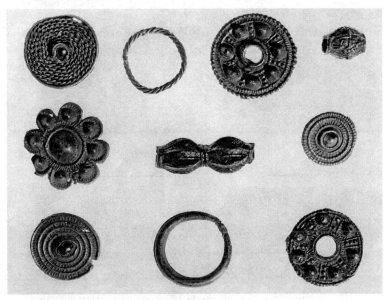

11 *Pewter rings and brooches, found in Cheapside, the unfinished stock of a London jeweller. A fragment of a brooch found in Dublin was manufactured from the same mould.* Courtesy Museum of London

12 Above *Tenth-century sock from Coppergate, York, made in a technique known as nålebinding, or needle-binding, using a coarse needle and a length of plied yarn, which in appearance looks like close-textured crochet work. This technique is still well known in Scandinavia, and is the only clear Scandinavian textile found in York. A similar example is known from a textile fragment from a Viking burial at Heath Wood, Ingleby. Courtesy York Archaeological Trust*

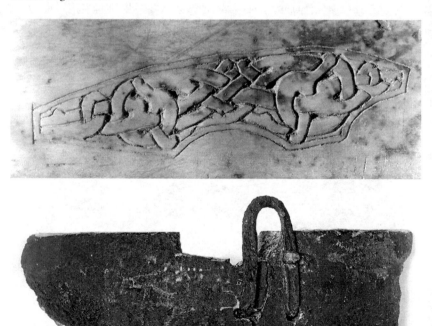

5cm

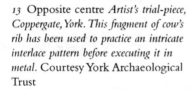

13 Opposite centre *Artist's trial-piece, Coppergate, York. This fragment of cow's rib has been used to practice an intricate interlace pattern before executing it in metal.* Courtesy York Archaeological Trust

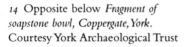

14 Opposite below *Fragment of soapstone bowl, Coppergate, York.* Courtesy York Archaeological Trust

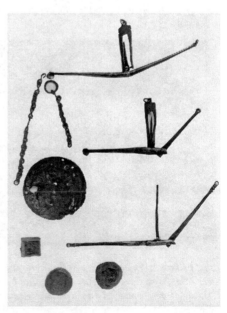

15 Above *Coins of the Scandinavian kings of York. Top: Anlaf Guthfrithsson, died 941 (raven); bottom left: Cnut, died 902 (cross); bottom right: Sihtric, died 927 (sword).* Courtesy York Archaeological Trust

16 Above right *Coin-manufacturing evidence, Coppergate, York.* Courtesy York Archaeological Trust

17 Right *Balances and weights, Coppergate, York. The upper one, still with a pan, has fixed arms; the other two have folding arms. Three lead weights are at bottom left.* Courtesy York Archaeological Trust

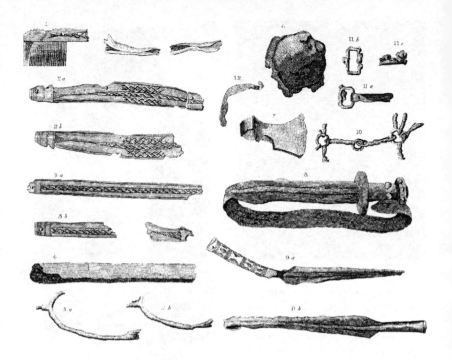

18 Viking grave finds, Hesket in the Forest (Cumbria). This nineteenth-century illustration shows: 1-3, antler comb fragments; 4, whetstone; 5, spurs; 6, shield boss; 7, axe; 8, sword; 9, spearheads; 10, bridle; 11, buckles; 12, iron fragment

19 St Martin's, Wharram Percy. In the churchyard, south of the chancel, the burials of two adults and a child were discovered. They were marked by limestone slabs, with head- and foot-stones. The child's grave contained a bone pin and a copper-alloy hook. Courtesy Wharram Research Project

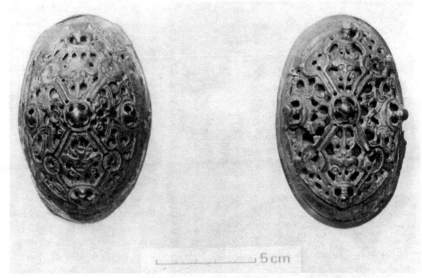

_____ 5 cm

20 Above *Oval
brooches, Bedale,
North Yorkshire.
Oval brooches are
characteristic finds
from Scandinavian
female graves; they
were worn on the
shoulders or breast
to hold together the
back and front of a
tunic.* Courtesy York
Archaeological
Trust

21 Right *Viking
Age graves under
York Minster. The
slabs and headstones
are decorated with
Scandinavian style
ornament.* © Crown
Copyright

22 Top *Grave slab, York Minster, apparently depicting the Germanic hero Sigurd about to stab the dragon Fafnir. This pagan scene may have been chosen for its heroic Christian parallels; the bow-shaped funerary monument can be seen as related to the full hogback forms. The monument was found in place over the grave of one of York's Anglo-Scandinavian elite.* © Crown Copyright

23 Centre *Hogback tombstones, Brompton, North Yorkshire. A total of eleven hogbacks were found built into the walls of the church when it was rebuilt in 1867. Having sold all the demolition debris to the builder the church was forced to buy five of the stones back. The Brompton hogbacks have magnificent end beasts, and may well be amongst the earliest in the country.* Courtesy Department of Archaeology, University of Durham

24 Bottom *Cross fragment, Weston church, North Yorkshire. The Weston Cross depicts a warrior wearing a short tunic who holds a sword and thrusts back a female figure. It typifies the Viking secular takeover of sculpture as it was carved out of an earlier Anglian cross, preserving the knotwork from the original lower arm, but re-cutting the upper part of the shaft for the figural scene.* Courtesy York Archaeological Trust

25 *The Cuerdale Hoard (Lancashire) was discovered in 1840 in a lead-lined chest by workmen clearing the banks of the River Ribble. It is the largest Viking Age hoard ever found in the British Isles, totalling some 40kg of silver. Estimates of its value today range between £300,000 and £4m. It originally comprised some 7500 coins, comprising c.5000 Viking issues, c.1000 Anglo-Saxon coins, and c.1000 Continental issues, including Frankish, Italian and Arabic coins. There were also some 1000 pieces of bullion silver, including c.350 ingots, and Irish arm-rings. The Carolingian coins were probably derived from Viking raids on France in the 890s and the Netherlands in 902. The Irish arm rings, in good condition, were the most recent additions to the hoard, but there were also some new York coins. It has been suggested that it was buried c.905 by Irish Norse exiles who, having been ejected from Dublin, needed a base in Britain from which they could campaign against the Yorkshire Danes. The Ribble estuary would have provided a natural haven for a Dublin fleet in exile (Graham Campbell ed. 1992).* Courtesy of the Board and Trustees of the British Museum

26 The Edda, *a full scale replica of the Oseberg ship, during one of her earliest trials under sail in 1988. The Oseberg ship had been used as a burial ship for a Norwegian princess, and was excavated in 1904. It was 21.75m long by 5.1m wide, with 15 pairs of oars. It may have been built, c.800, as some form of high performance 'royal yacht'.* Courtesy M.O.H.Carver and D.Lee

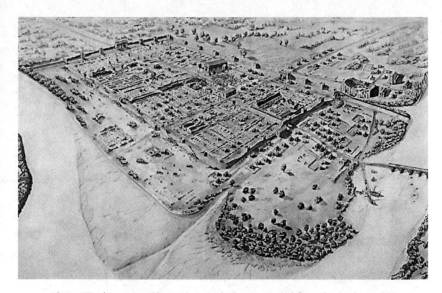

28 Above *Tenth-century Chester as it might have appeared from the south-west. The defences of the Roman fortress remain substantially intact but are believed to have been extended from the north-western and south-eastern corners to the river Dee after the establishment of the Æthelflaedan burh. (Painting by students of Blackpool and Fylde College: David Astley, Andrew Beckett and Carl Flint).* Copyright Chester City Council

29 Right *Green Shiel, Lindisfarne: Building C in the course of excavation.* Courtesy D. O'Sullivan

27 Opposite below *Artist's reconstruction of a York quayside scene.* Courtesy Yorkshire Museum

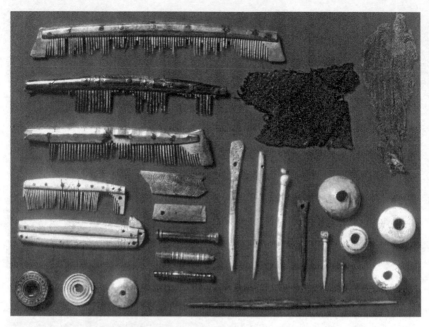

30 Above *Tenth-century bone and antler combs, spindlewhorls, needles and textile fragments, York.* Courtesy York Archaeological Trust

31 Centre *Tenth-century silver- and lead-alloy disc brooches, Coppergate, York.* Courtesy York Archaeological Trust

32 Below *Two Anglo-Scandinavian bells, Cottam (East Yorkshire)*

33 St Martin's, Wharram Percy.
*Excavation of the interior of the church
of the deserted medieval village revealed
a typical sequence of development of a
parish church. In the mid to late tenth
century a small timber church was
constructed, represented only by post-
holes. This was replaced in the early
to mid eleventh century by a small
two-celled stone structure, represented
by the wide foundation trenches in
the photograph. The church continued
to grow until the fourteenth century.*
Courtesy Wharram Research
Project

34 *Heath Wood, Ingleby: Mound 50 under excavation. The mound contained cremated
human and animal remains and a variety of burnt grave offerings*

35 *Watercolour of Viking grave-goods, Claugton Hall, Lancashire. The Viking Age finds comprised a pair of gilt copper alloy oval brooches, apparently wrapped up back-to-back in cloth and encasing two beads, a Carolingian silver mount and a tooth, and various iron objects, including a sword, spear, axe and hammer. This may have been a double burial of male and female, but it is more likely that the burial was male and the brooches formed a ritual deposit of various amulets.* Courtesy Society of Antiquaries

36 *Grave slab from St Paul's Cathedral churchyard, London. The rectangular slab shows a dragon-like beast, originally coloured dark blue, with the details picked out in brown and white.* Courtesy Museum of London

At Sashes (Berkshire) a fort was established on an island in the Thames. Many of these *burhs* were small in extent or low in relief, but made use of natural defences such as marshland, streams or steep slopes, and therefore had an irregular plan. The main access was usually from one direction only, and this was where the man-made defences were constructed. Lydford was sited on a wedge-shaped promontory; it was flanked by a gorge on two sides, and a narrow valley on the third; the exposed side was defended by a bank *c.*12m wide and a ditch 200m in length, with a central gate.

Elsewhere, new towns were created on open sites, and provided with rectangular perimeter defences modelled on Roman forts. This group comprises Cricklade (Wiltshire), Oxford, Wallingford (Oxfordshire), and Wareham (Dorset). These *burhs* were often established on river sites, either controlling a river crossing, as at Wallingford, or where the river ceased to be navigable, as at Cricklade.

Burhs were also sited where there was already a concentration of settlement, such as around an estate centre or minster church (see chapter 9), as at Cricklade, Malmesbury, Shaftesbury, Wareham or Wilton. These were already proto-urban sites, providing a focus for a non-agricultural population and acting as administrative, fiscal, religious and ceremonial centres, frequently with the association of a royal palace and minster church.

The Saxon defences follow a common pattern. The ramparts were of damp construction, initially of clay or clay and turves, with varying amounts of wooden reinforcement. They were scarped at the front and sloped at the rear; a height of 2-3m and a width of 9-12m were normal; presumably they were crowned with timber palisades. This first defensive phase is usually assumed to be Ælfredian, although the archaeological evidence usually only proves that they are post-Roman, and they could have been constructed before Ælfred's reign. At many burhs there is a second rampart phase, in which a stone wall was added to the bank to replace the timber palisade in the late tenth or early eleventh centuries. At Cadbury (Somerset), a late *burh*, an earthen bank was erected over the rampart of the Iron Age hillfort and faced with a mortared masonry wall in a single operation. A substantial stone gatehouse was built at the south-west entrance; it has been suggested that a timber bridge carried a wall walk over the entrance, but there is no evidence for anything other than a monumental arch and massive timber gates. Cadbury appears to have been founded as an emergency measure between *c.*1010-20, designed to put at least one English mint in a place of safety. In its interior the foundation trenches were dug for a cruciform church, but the church was never built as the site was abandoned on the defeat of Æthelred (Alcock 1995).

Beyond the rampart it is likely that most *burhs* were also defended by a sequence of ditches, following the Roman fashion. These have been observed at Wareham, Cricklade, Lydford, Oxford and Twynham. At Cricklade an elaborate triple ditch system comprised two smaller ditches and a wide outer ditch outside the rampart, separated from it by a 6m wide berm. This may have been the standard pattern, although excavations have rarely uncovered such an extensive area.

Finally, it appears that the defences of some *burhs* were razed in the eleventh century. At Cricklade, Lydford, South Cadbury and Wareham the walls were systematically destroyed and the ditches filled in, probably at the command of Knutr in order to consolidate his position after he became king in 1016.

Within the walls, evidence for deliberate and regular town planning has been recovered from those burhs which were established as permanent settlements. Land ownership was as much an issue in the towns as it was in the countryside; rectilinear street systems and property boundaries testify to the laying out of individual tenements under private ownership. Land was parcelled out, initially in large blocks, each representing small estates. As towns became more successful these plots were subdivided, each division retaining a valuable bit of street front, the tenements developing into long narrow strips. At first, however, many *burhs* may have still contained many open spaces; areas of Chicester, Cricklade, Twynham, Wallingford and Wareham retained a rural character well into the tenth century.

At Winchester the rectilinear street plan was laid out in the 880s or early 890s. It has been calculated that there were some 8.6km (5.4 miles) of streets in Winchester, requiring some 8,000 tonnes of flint cobbles to surface them. The High Street provided a major east-west thoroughfare; a single back street running parallel to the High Street on either side of it provided access to the rear of the properties. There were also regularly spaced north-south streets at right angles to the High Street and an intra-mural wall street. This last feature is not found in Roman towns, but was integral with the laying out of the *burhs*. In Winchester and Lydford individual tenements were marked by ditches; in Durham, Oxford, and York, wattle fences seem to have been the norm. It has been demonstrated that the systematic division of land associated with the laying out of the *burhs* was frequently conducted on the basis of a 4-pole unit (where 1 pole = 5m), and these units have been observed at Chichester, Colchester, Cricklade, London, Wareham, and Wallingford as well as Winchester.

The fortified *burhs* provided not only a haven for trade and industry but also a market for its products, and for materials and produce imported from the hinterland. Corn driers at Wallingford demonstrate that it functioned as an agricultural centre, perhaps a market town. Lydford may have been set up as a market centre for tin from Dartmoor. Axbridge, Langport and Watchet each developed as small defended markets for adjacent royal estates. Winchester, unlike the earlier *Hamwic*, was part of a ranked hierarchy of markets, although it was the only major *burh* in Hampshire; others may have been deliberately suppressed to remove competition. Streams running through the town provided useful resources for industry. By the end of the tenth century a number of specialised activities had developed in different sectors, reflected in street names like Tanner Street, Fleshmonger Street, and Shieldwright Street. The south-east quarter appears to have been a royal and ecclesiastical centre; a stone-built tower set in an enclosure on Brook Street may have been a residential compound of an elite group, its architecture reflecting their classical aspirations.

The same spatial concentration of specialist crafts has been observed in York. In some cases the siting of industries may have been governed by the need for natural resources, such as water for tanning, but others may reflect an act of deliberate planning and organisation. Markets were generally held outside the walls. At Cricklade there is evidence for a market place outside the west gate; in York the Scandinavian name Bootham may represent the position of market booths outside the city walls.

THE FIVE BOROUGHS

There is some evidence for a well-defined group of towns in the East Midlands, within the area of the Danelaw settled by the Viking Great Army. They are listed in the Anglo-Saxon Chronicle entry for 942 as comprising Derby, Leicester, Lincoln, Nottingham and Stamford (9), although there is also a reference to Seven Boroughs, perhaps including Manchester, and Doncaster or Torksey.

It was once believed that the Five Boroughs were specially fortified towns, established as an act of Danish policy after the partitions of 876-7, and used by Ælfred as a model for the Wessex *burhs*. However, they may not have become Danish strongholds until 910-20, which would mean that they were modelled upon the Wessex *burhs*, rather than vice versa (Hall 1989).

The sites have a number of features in common, including their position on navigable rivers or important prehistoric or Roman land routes. Derby (Little Chester), Leicester and Lincoln had each been Roman fortifications. In Leicester the Viking Age defences probably utilised the Roman walls and ditches. In Lincoln the Roman walls continued to define a defended area, although there is no evidence for Viking Age modification. Certainly many Roman buildings were still standing in the ninth century and some were demolished when the Viking Age town was built.

By comparison with the *burhs* of Wessex, the Five Boroughs were on the small to medium size. Derby may have been 29ha (65 acres); Lincoln 38ha (85 acres) if the Roman town was extended down to the river. Nottingham was 13.75ha (31 acres), and at Stamford the northern *burh* covered only 6ha (13 acres) and the southern one 3.75ha (8.5 acres).

All have traces of Middle Saxon occupation, probably as estate centres. In Derby (or Northworthy, as it was known before the Vikings changed its name), St Alkmund's Church was probably a Saxon minster associated with a royal or ecclesiastical estate centre. In Leicester, a Saxon minster church at Jewry Wall seems to have incorporated upstanding Roman masonry. In Lincoln there is evidence for activity in widely spread parts of the city from the fifth to the ninth centuries. The church of St Paul-in-the-Bail represents the continued existence of a religious centre in the heart of the Roman fortress.

At Nottingham and Stamford there is some evidence for Middle Saxon enclosures which pre-date the Viking takeover. The Viking army is described as wintering in a fortress at Nottingham in 868. In 918 Nottingham was captured by Edward, and two years later he built a second *burh* on the south bank of the River Trent opposite the Viking *burh*, connecting the two with a bridge. The northern *burh* was defended by a major ditch some 6m wide by 3.5m deep. This had been recut at least once during the Viking Age, and the flattened U profile changed to a V, although it is not known exactly when.

At Stamford there is evidence of three concentric ditches below the bailey of the Norman castle, the innermost with a timber palisade. They enclosed an area of 1.1ha (2.5 acres),

which is only about twice the size of the Viking fort at
Repton, but could represent a Saxon estate centre similar to
that at Goltho (see chapter 3), a Viking temporary raiding
base, or a Viking or Edwardian *burh*. The latter is more likely
to be represented by a second defended enclosure recognised
north of the Welland. The Anglo-Saxon Chronicle records
the submission of the Vikings in the northern *burh* in 918 and
the construction of a second *burh* on the south bank, where
another small enclosure has been found, as at Nottingham.

Whilst the Five Boroughs may have been occupied in
the Middle Saxon period, none were urban sites before the
Viking Age, although it has been suggested that the urban
element was created by Edward the Elder in the early tenth
century within the captured Viking fortresses.

So far there has been little success in finding Viking Age
archaeological remains within Derby, although a cess pit and
rubble platform have been excavated within the Roman fort
at Little Chester, on the opposite bank of the Derwent, which
may have been the Viking base (Hall 1974). In Leicester
the Southgate Street pottery kiln of the late tenth century
suggests the town was a manufacturing and commercial
centre, but no other evidence has so far been found.

The best evidence for urban activity within the Five
Boroughs comes from Lincoln, where there was riverside
activity and land reclamation in the tenth century, and
evidence for the establishment of a new street system on the
Flaxengate and Michaelgate sites some time after the Viking
takeover in 874. This lacks the regularity of the Wessex *burhs*,
but still represents a planned development. The Flaxengate
site must have been under common ownership as extensive
levelling dumps must represent coordinated building

programmes. The earliest buildings were laid out with their long axes parallel to the street, perhaps suggesting that there was less pressure for space in Lincoln than elsewhere. Late ninth- and tenth-century buildings have also been excavated at Hungate and Michaelgate. However, sustained growth within Lincoln largely postdates the initial Viking settlement. The Flaxengate area may have received an initial boost in the late ninth century, but its real boom as an industrial centre belongs almost a century later, to the period *c.*960-1070, and especially *c.*960-1010 with the growth of the Lincoln mint. It was then that glass and copper-alloy working assumed industrial proportions with specialised workshops, and the Flaxengate development was extended into Grantham Street (Perring 1981).

In Nottingham a number of Viking Age structures have been encountered at Drury Hill, Fishergate and Woolpack Lane, and pottery was being manufactured at Halifax Place. It has been argued, however, that urbanisation did not take place until *c.*925-50, and industrialization not until *c.*1000.

In Stamford timber buildings have been found fronting onto the High Street, with wooden fences dividing one property from the next. Iron smelting and pottery production were important industries during the Viking Age, although both were dependent upon the rural hinterland for their raw materials. A grain-drying kiln found within the fortified enclosure beneath the medieval castle also suggests close links with the countryside. Within Stamford industrial activity was fairly loosely zoned, as at Thetford, and in contrast to Ipswich and Norwich where the potters were concentrated in one place (Carter 1978; Mahany 1982; Mahany and Roffe 1983).

Thus, although Scandinavians may have been responsible for establishing the Five Boroughs as fortified sites which, like the Wessex *burhs*, would develop into trading and industrial centres, it is unclear how far they were responsible for the development of town life within them.

There are possible Viking foundations at a number of other sites, including Thetford and Northampton. The town of Thetford was occupied from the ninth to the eleventh or early twelfth centuries. It may have been an earlier Anglo-Saxon royal or ecclesiastical estate centre, but was used as a wintering place for the Danish army in 869-70, and this appears to have provided the main impetus for its development, with the earliest dating evidence provided by a little Stamford ware of the late ninth century. Thetford is connected by river to the Wash and the North Sea, and this favoured its growth as a trading town. The first defences were constructed on the south bank of the Little Ouse. Initially the interior was not fully occupied but settlement expanded rapidly until it extended beyond the line of the defences in the late tenth century, eventually occupying an irregular area of some 60ha (135 acres) south of the river, and a further area of 15ha (34 acres) to the north. The establishment of a bridgehead to control the river crossing is reminiscent of both Nottingham and Stamford.

The interior of the town was divided up into a number of properties demarcated by long boundary ditches, although the street frontages were not built up. Both sunken and surface buildings were erected within the properties, wells were sunk, and rubbish pits were dug along the boundaries. The dividing up or amalgamation of properties was common, but the town retained an open plan and was never fully built up. It was originally suggested that industrial activity was zoned within the town, but later work has been less conclusive, with only the pottery kilns definitely concentrated in the north-west. Thetford gained a mint but never became an international trading port, and never imported pottery from the Continent. The town had declined by the Norman Conquest; the settlement south of the river was deserted in favour of the smaller settlement to the north (Dallas 1992; Dunmore and Carr 1976; Rogerson and Dallas 1984).

In Northampton, Middle Saxon occupation was restricted to an area of some 20ha (45 acres) around St Peter's church where a minster and palace may have acted as the centre of a royal estate. At St Peter's Street a timber hall was superceded by a massive stone hall of Carolingian style *c.*820-75. This building may have been the centre of a royal estate which was broken up during the Danish settlement, although John Blair has argued that it is a minster church, rather than a royal palace (Blair 1996). It is possible that the stone hall was abandoned, and demolished, as a direct result of Danish occupation.

There is nothing in Northampton to imply urban status before the late ninth century. There was a dramatic inten-sification of activity, however, during the period of Danish occupation, between the late ninth century and the arrival of Edward the Elder in 917. An area of around 24ha (59 acres) was enclosed by a wide ditch. Within this area there is no evidence for the deliberate laying out of a street plan but a number of buildings were erected in a fairly loose settlement pattern, comparable to that at Thetford. In the tenth century the town became the base for a large number of craftworkers, including those working in iron, copper and silver, bone and antler, and textiles. Although the site may have initially been chosen by the Danes as a military base, it rapidly developed into a town (Williams 1979; 1984).

Having examined the towns of Viking Age England, what was the Scandinavian contribution to urbanism? The ninth and tenth centuries were times of urban expansion in England, even outside the areas of Viking influence. In the Isle of Man, which was devoid of towns, the Vikings founded no urban centres. In Ireland they imported an English form of town. In York the Vikings may have contributed to the growth of the urban community, but are unlikely to have created it. Only in the case of Derby was the English name for the town changed to a Scandinavian one. Nonetheless, the Vikings did provide an indirect stimulus to urban growth both in the defended sites which they set up, and perhaps more importantly, in those maintained against them.

The transition from *wics* to *burhs* reflects a fundamental change in the economic system. In the eighth century one means by which Anglo-Saxon kings maintained royal power was by restricting the activities of foreign traders and levying tolls on controlled exchange in *wics*. As power was consolidated amongst a few kingdoms there was a growing need for systems of administration and control. The role of kings in the development of towns was partly passive; royal minsters and estate administrative centres provided nuclei for settlements, markets and craftsmen. But the kings of Mercia and Wessex were also active in promoting the growth of towns. The *burhs* were instigated as a system of national defence, but they also had an economic role as market centres. Their ramparts excluded enemies, but also provided a means of regulating comings and goings. Royal attempts to control trade and channel it through these foundations were facilitated by the proliferation of a stable, royal controlled coinage. The First Law Code of Edward the Elder decreed that 'no one shall buy or sell except in a market town with the witness of the port-reeve and of other men of credit'. Æthelstan's Second Code stated that 'no one shall buy goods worth more than 20 pence, outside a town; but he shall buy within the town, in the presence of the port-reeve or some other trustworthy man'. As towns developed, specialisation in crafts and trades increased, and the size of the non-agricultural population which had to be supported by the rural hinterland grew. The seizure of the countryside by Scandinavian settlers may have caused some of the rural dispossessed to seek new opportunities in towns. It may not be coincidence that the fastest growing ninth-century towns were in those areas most affected by Scandinavian land-taking.

5

THE BUILT ENVIRONMENT

Successive invasions of England have often led to sweeping changes in the appearance of settlements as the immigrants imported their preferred style of dwelling. For the Viking Age, however, it is difficult to identify any specifically Scandinavian-style buildings in England. There are no true long-houses with cattle byres at one end and dwelling space at the other, for example, such as have been excavated in Denmark. In York, the Viking town-houses seem no different from what we would expect of the Anglo-Saxons; indeed it is impossible to say that the Coppergate buildings were home to Scandinavian rather than Anglo-Saxon craftsmen. There was also little regional variation, with differences being mainly determined by the availability of raw materials such as wood and stone, rather than cultural differences. Rather than expecting to detect Scandinavian influence by examination of excavated buildings, it may be more realistic to look for new building forms corresponding to new socio-economic relations (Batey 1995; Richards 2000).

TIMBER BUILDINGS

Over most of lowland England, timber was used for most secular buildings from the end of the Roman period until after the Norman Conquest. Stone was used for the construction of some important churches from the seventh century onwards, and by Ælfred's time some royal residences were built of stone, but although it might be used for ancillary features, such as porches, it rarely had a structural role in either urban or rural housing. Indeed, the Old English verb used to refer to construction work in early documents is normally *timbran*.

Timber buildings may be classified into two main categories, according to whether they are ground-level or sunken structures (Rahtz 1976). Ground-level buildings are found in both town and country, but unlike the Early Anglo-Saxon period, when it was common to find sunken workshops in most rural settlements, by the Viking Age the sunken buildings are found almost exclusively in towns, where they are often in equal numbers to the surface buildings. In London, for example, of traces of over 50 buildings of the ninth to the twelfth centuries, 60 per cent were ground level structures, and 40 per cent were sunken.

GROUND-LEVEL BUILDINGS

A basic style of single-storey town house and workshop has now been identified in many Viking Age towns. In London the ground-level buildings are usually found with their gable ends fronting onto the streets, such as at Bow Lane, Botolph

Lane and Milk Street. They are generally 4-5m wide, following the width of the tenement plots, with a greater variation in length, ranging from 6.5-10m. Most contained only one room; they had doors in the side and gable walls (Horsman *et al.* 1988). At Coppergate, York, and Flaxengate, Lincoln, the houses again occupied the street frontage plots. At Lincoln, there was some evidence for internal partitioning with a cross passage joining opposing doors in the middle of the long sides, following the rural fashion.

More substantial timber halls have been excavated at high-status sites such as Cheddar, Faccombe Netherton, Goltho, North Elmham, Portchester and Raunds. The use of internal aisle posts to partition the interior of the larger halls into three aisles has been recognised at many of these sites. A substantial eleventh-century hall, 15 x 7.5m, has been excavated at Waltham Abbey (Essex). The hall has been described as Viking, although there is nothing specifically Scandinavian about it. The position of the aisle posts was marked by clay foundations, but there was no trace of timber wall posts apart from continuous foundation trenches. It has been suggested that the hall had turf walls, but there is little evidence to support this interpretation (Huggins 1976). At Sulgrave, the eleventh-century timber-framed hall was erected on stone footings. It was divided into five bays, with a cobbled porch at one end and a central hearth. The service end, from which the meal was brought, was screened off, whilst at the other end there was a two-storeyed chamber block. A detached timber building near the porch has been interpreted as the kitchen.

BOW-SIDED HALLS

A particular class of rectangular timber halls with bowed walls is often linked with Viking influence. In fact they are part of a long building tradition which has a wide distribution, although they are associated particularly with Viking Age Denmark, and are also found in most of the areas settled by Scandinavians or under their direct influence. They are frequently identified as the houses of the rural aristocracy and the building style may have been popular with a particular class of secular landowners which happened to be dominated by Scandinavians, rather than being specifically Viking.

Various theories have been propounded to explain their bow-sided plan. They are certainly not derived from upturned ships, as was once suggested; nor can they have been designed to provide protection against the wind, although the bow-sided structure does give some extra stability.

In England bow-sided halls have been found at Buckden (Huntingdonshire), Catholme, Cheddar, Goltho and Sulgrave, and there are smaller buildings which also have bowed sides at Chester, Durham, Nottingham and Thetford. A bow-sided building at St Neots, with a planked floor over timber joists resting on sill beams has been interpreted as a granary, although it may simply be a medium-sized quality residence.

The ninth-century bow-sided halls at Cheddar and Goltho are both of similar plan and dimensions, 24m long by 6m wide at the centre. In each case the wall posts were set in trenches, with evidence for stave walls at Goltho. At Cheddar the presence of double wall posts with the inner one sloping inwards has led to the suggestion that there was an upper storey whose floor was supported by the inner posts. At Goltho there was evidence that the hall was divided into three rooms, with a raised dais at one end and a cobbled hearth in the centre of the dais. Each hall had three doorways: at Goltho there was one at the east end of the hall, and one either side of the antechamber; at Cheddar there was also a pair of opposed doorways at one end of the hall, but the third appears to have provided access to the upper storey.

SUNKEN BUILDINGS

Sunken buildings are easy to recognise archaeologically as rectangular cuts into the ground surface. In London traces of at least 17 sunken buildings have been excavated dating from the late ninth to the late eleventh centuries, and ranging between 2.8-5.6m wide and 4.2 13.4m long. There is also considerable variation in depth, between 0.41-2.3m, and it is possible to distinguish between two types of sunken buildings.

The first group, such as that excavated at Milk Street, have a floor *c.*0.5-1m below the ground level, and may be described as sunken-floored buildings. At Milk Street the upcast earth was piled against the outside wall and grassed over, providing a wall up to 1m wide, and much like the stone and turf walls at sites such as Hound Tor and Hutholes in appearance. Another example is known from Lower Bridge Street, Chester, where Building 4 had a sunken floor only 0.84m below the ground surface, and must have been a single-storeyed semi-sunken building. Such sunken-floored buildings are known from the late ninth century onwards.

The second category of sunken building has a floor at *c*.1-2.5m below the contemporary ground surface, and is more accurately described as a cellared building. These structures are often also distinguished by double linings of horizontal planks affixed to either side of the wall posts, and may have joisted floors. In York this new style of sunken building was introduced across the Coppergate site within a decade of 970, replacing the post-and-wattle structures (Hall 1982; 1984). In London too, their introduction has been dated to the late tenth and early eleventh centuries. These deep cellared buildings are invariably found away from the street frontages in London. No evidence of a hearth has been found in the cellars, which presumably must have been used for storage below a ground-level dwelling and workshop. At Wallingford and Oxford cellared buildings were laid out along the major street frontages by the early eleventh century (Hassall 1986). At Lower Bridge Street, Chester, three almost identical examples have been excavated (Mason 1985). Each had a length-breadth ratio of 5:4 and was some 1.7-1.8m deep, with the lower metre cut into solid bedrock. Post-holes indicated the position of timber walls around the cellars. The floors were planked across at ground level, with access to the cellar down a flight of steps from the outside. At Thetford there were traces of struts sloping inwards that could have supported the upper floor. At York there was no structural evidence for an upper storey but the need to increase the usable space provides the best explanation for the introduction of a cellar, and the comparative evidence from London and Chester suggests that it was likely. A raised first floor could also have contained a clay-lined hearth, conspicuously absent from the basements.

Sunken buildings are almost exclusively an urban phenomenon in the Viking Age, and must have been built in response
to particular needs. The sunken-floored type can be seen as
developing out of a native tradition, introduced into England
by the Anglo-Saxons. They appear to have been mainly used
as urban workshops, although there are a few rural examples,
such as the ninth-century sunken-floored bread oven at
Fladbury (Hereford and Worcester). The cellared buildings
appear to be a response to developments within urban
communities arising in the second half of the tenth century,
probably the need to store goods in transit, or stock-in-trade.
The cellars would have provided cool and secure repositories
for foodstuffs and other supplies, and appear to be associated with the tenth-century revival of trade and growth of
trading towns (see chapter 6). Cellared buildings also appear
in Danish towns such as Århus in the tenth century, but it
is not clear if they represent a Scandinavian introduction to
England or are simply part of a general north-west European
development.

FOUNDATIONS

Timber-framing, by which buildings are constructed around
a timber frame held together by carpentered joints, was not
widely used in England until after the Norman Conquest.
The structural stability of Viking Age buildings therefore
generally depended upon their foundation methods. The
most common technique was to use earth-fast foundations.
In some cases, as for the peasant houses at North Elmham
and Barton Blount, the wall posts might still be set directly

in the ground. In towns too, such as Lincoln and York, this was common practice, with posts sometimes driven into the ground as stakes, but more usually placed in post-holes packed with stones. Such posts often do not appear to have been set in pairs, but may sometimes have just acted as stiffeners for substantial cob or clay walls.

Increasingly, however, a continuous trench was dug along the wall lines, and the vertical posts or staves set within it, following a technique developed at Middle Saxon sites such as Chalton and Maxey. During the Viking Age this 'post-in-trench' technique was utilised for major buildings at Cheddar, Goltho, Middle Harling (Norfolk), Portchester and North Elmham. At Catholme side walls were set in trenches, whilst the gable ends were supported by individual posts. Alternatively, individual post-pits could be excavated to hold massive vertical timbers, each up to 0.6m across, for substantial structures such as the West Hall at Cheddar.

During the Viking Age a new foundation technique of using a 'sill beam' was introduced at urban sites such as Chester, York and London, and in rural settings such as Buckden, North Elmham, Northolt (Middlesex), Portchester, St Neots, Sulgrave and Waltham Abbey. A sill beam is a horizontal beam which may be set in a foundation trench, or placed directly on the ground surface. The wall posts rest upon it, and may be held in position by a raised timber lip or sill, or they may be set into the beam in rectangular sockets. At Coppergate, York, massive oak beams, up to 7m long, with raised sills, were set in cuts up to 1.5m deep as the foundations of the planked sunken buildings.

Another new technique, first used in the mid-tenth or early eleventh century in London, was to employ a foundation bed, such as a rubble platform or stone pads, to support the structural timbers. In London, the development of mortar or stone sills represents an attempt at prolonging the life of timber buildings, and thereby making more effective use of the woodland resource (Milne 1992). At Flaxengate, Lincoln, one building rested upon a single course of stone footings which may have supported a raised plank floor to lift perishable materials such as grain off the damp ground.

WALLS

The most common walling material at the start of the Viking Age was probably wattlework, following a long Anglo-Saxon tradition. In York in the first half of the tenth century post-and-wattle was the standard method of building construction (*plate 6*). At neither York nor Lincoln, however, has clay daub been found on the walls, and the small quantities present suggest it may only have been lining clay ovens. Clay and straw may also have been used to make cob walls. It is likely that fur or textile drapes may have been used to cut out draughts. In York, screens of woven willow twigs may have been used to provide wall insulation, or may have fallen from the loft.

Wattlework was inappropriate, however, as a walling material for the new class of sunken buildings, as it would have collapsed under the pressure of the surrounding earth. At both London and York wall cladding for the sunken buildings was provided by post-and-plank construction. At York the wall posts, carefully squared and regularly spaced at short intervals, supported layers of horizontal oak planks which were laid edge on edge (*plate 7*). There was no evidence for the use of pegs, nails or joints in the lower 1.75m of the walls; apparently the planks were held in place against the wall posts by the sill beam and the weight of surrounding earth. These posts appear to have been paired across the building and so were presumably held upright by tie-beams spanning the width of the building at the top of the walls. There are also instances of an inner skin of horizontal planks being fastened to the wall posts to provide a cavity wall.

Staves, or vertically set planks, first appear in London in the eleventh century, but have now been found earlier at other sites, such as Goltho, where half sections of trees, about 0.45m wide, were set in a trench with their curving face outwards. The method is well known from Norwegian stave churches, and was adopted at St Andrew's, Greensted-juxta-Ongar (Essex), although there is no evidence that its adoption in England was due to Scandinavian influence. At Goltho the two structural traditions of stave and post construction persisted side by side until after the Norman Conquest.

Any available wood seems to have been used for wall construction, with a clear preponderance of hazel for wattle-work and oak for wall posts and planks, with willow, alder and birch in descending order of importance. Where joints needed to be fixed then wooden pegs appear to have been used more commonly than iron nails. The standard mortise and tenon joint was unknown before the Norman Conquest. In contrast to the use of elaborate joinery in late medieval structures it is clear that the builders of Viking Age houses and workshops invested a minimum of labour and skill in these structures (Milne 1992).

ROOFS, FLOORS AND INTERNAL FITTINGS

For the smaller buildings roofs generally rested directly upon the walls, although for larger halls such as those at Cheddar and North Elmham their weight appears to have been borne by internal posts. Straw and hay may have been used for thatching, or in some areas turves may have been used. There is little evidence for wooden shingles although most of the hogback stones apparently have shingled roofs.

Floors were most commonly of beaten earth or clay, but sand, gravel, and mortar are also known. At Lincoln there was evidence of rushes and other grasses, and at Durham sedges, rushes, heather, bracken, meadowsweet and crowfoot were laid over the sand floor as a sweet-smelling covering which could be replaced before it became unpleasant. At Thetford the floor of one of the sunken buildings had been mortared; another was surfaced with closely packed cobbles. In York several buildings had plank floors resting on joints. At Coppergate the floor boards had been carefully cut to fit flush around the internal wall posts so as to lap against the wall.

Ground-level buildings generally had at least two entrances, sometimes protected by a wooden porch, as at Portchester. The basements of sunken buildings could have been entered by an internal ladder, but many were entered directly from outside. In Ipswich, London, and at the Clarendon Hotel site, Oxford, earthen steps have been identified in shallow extensions. At Thetford the cellar of Building J was approached down a 5m long ramp revetted with posts. At Coppergate the sunken buildings were entered from the rear along sunken passageways revetted with stone, but may also have had a second entrance at the street front. At Chester each of the sunken buildings had a ramped extension some 2.5m long cut into the solid rock. These would have been dangerously steep unless provided with a flight of wooden steps, and were probably covered by a porch to keep out the rain.

All buildings must have been provided with wooden doors, although they are rarely found. In London, one was found lying in demolition debris. It comprised four vertical oak boards secured by diagonal battens on inner face and fastened together with iron nails. The remains of iron hinges were also found. Various Viking Age lock mechanisms have been excavated, but these are generally supposed to have originated from chests rather than doors.

There is evidence for window glass from two London sunken buildings, but glass is otherwise rare with no traces even on aristocratic sites such as Goltho, although it may normally have been robbed as a precious commodity. From Coppergate the remains of a possible window shutter have been recovered. Internal lighting would have been provided by the hearth fire, and by small oil lamps. In the tenth and early eleventh centuries there are stone and pottery oil lamps with bases splayed to sit on the floor or in a niche on the wall.

All buildings normally had a central hearth, usually consisting of baked clay over a bed of stone. Pottery cooking vessels would be set in the embers. In York a number of industrial hearths, up to 1.2 x 1.8m, were found positioned in the centre of the floor, and built one upon the other as the floor level rose. They had a clay base, of which only a small part was normally burnt, surrounded by a kerb of limestone blocks, reused Roman tile, or wooden beams. Specialist kitchen buildings such as that at Goltho were often provided with ovens built of baked clay and wattle on a stone rubble base; in one London example the clay walls were supported by 33 angled stakes. At Portchester one even had a clay dome set on a base of reused Roman tile and lumps of limestone set in clay.

Many buildings presumably had internal timber fittings such as wall benches and beds, although remains are more common in stone buildings, where they survive incorporated in the stone structures. At Coppergate one building had rows of stakes running parallel to both side walls and 0.6m from the walls for two thirds of the excavated length of the building; these probably represent wattlework revetting for earth-packed wall benches. Substantial pits were dug inside some of the York buildings; one assumes that these were used for storage, and were originally covered by planks. Storage of valuables would have been undertaken in sturdy wooden chests, with perishable goods stored in pottery vessels. At Pudding Lane, London, two abandoned buildings had smashed fragments of large spouted storage jars on the floor.

The life expectancy of timber buildings generally appears to have been fairly short. From Cheddar, Lincoln, London and York there are consistent estimates for a lifespan of between 5 and 25 years, although one London example was still in use after 40. Floors could be resurfaced every 5-10 years, but wall posts set in earth may have quickly rotted. Fire seems to have been the major cause of destruction in towns, sweeping along rows of thatched houses and resulting in simultaneous redevelopment across a whole site. At Coppergate the positions of structures remain static for some 50 years, even though individual buildings were gutted by fire and totally rebuilt on several occasions. Developments in construction techniques appear to occur contemporaneously from tenement to tenement, suggesting that all four Coppergate tenements were under the control of one landlord, or that professional builders were hired to replace the street. At Saddler Street, Durham, and other sites, the primitive nature of wattle construction has suggested that these buildings were DIY affairs (Carver 1979). At aristocratic sites, however, where sophisticated stave and other techniques were employed we can assume that skilled craftsmen were responsible.

STONE BUILDINGS

In the upland zone of England, and in the south-west, stone was generally used as the basic building material, with wood reserved for the structural timbers and roof beams. In some areas this may have been determined by the shortage of suitable building timber compared with the availability of building stone, but this is not a full answer, and the reasons for the preference for stone may have been culturally as much as environmentally determined. Norse Vikings generally built their residences in stone, but the use of stone cannot be seen as a Viking trait in itself, as the native population in each of these areas also preferred stone.

The principal building at Ribblehead is in many respects a typical Norse dwelling, although in the absence of comparable sites it is impossible to determine if it is distinguishable in any way from pre-Viking buildings in the area (King 1978). The hall is some 19m long by 4m wide, with walls 1.5-1.8m thick (*8*). The outer wall faces were marked with a line of boulders and the inner ones constructed of coursed limestone slabs, with limestone rubble and earth used to provide the wall filling and insulation against draughts. A wicker lining could have been used to provide extra protection. Sandstone was used for the hearth and oven. There was a low bench against the west wall in the lower half of the building. The roof timbers apparently came all the way down to the ground at the outer edges of the wall. The roofs may have been thatched or covered with turves, and extended down to the ground. The gable ends were provided with central paved doorways, and the buildings were linked by stone pathways. A walled porch gave the kitchen building extra protection against the wind. Similar foundations of low stone walls were excavated at Simy Folds, although it was suggested that the walls may have been heightened with turf. Within the hall central paving would have provided footings for vertical posts which supported the ridge post for the rafters. The longhouses were the dwellings, with the smaller sub-rectangular buildings used for storage, as dairies or as workshops (Coggins *et al.* 1983).

At Green Shiel, Lindisfarne, two of the longhouses were each divided into two areas. One end may have been used for animals, and the other as a dwelling place, mirroring the divisions of later medieval peasant houses, but without the cross-passages which are typical of the later buildings. A third building was entered by a passage in the gable wall, leading directly into a series of compartments, each of which were probably individual byres (*plate 29*). Some of the rooms were paved with large flat slabs. The nearby beach seems to have been the source of the building stone; the walling is made from limestone which could have been quarried along the foreshore, with some large rounded beach pebbles. The ready availability of stone, rather than preference for a Scandinavian building tradition, is the obvious explanation for the choice of stone at Green Shiel instead of the more usual timber. The walls were crudely faced with irregular blocks with rubble infill; there is no trace of clay or mortar bonding. What the builders lacked in technique they made up for in stolidity; the outer walls were broad (up to 2m thick). In one of the buildings a line of post holes running down the centre provides the best indication of how the structures were roofed, suggesting a pitched thatched roof supported by central posts (O'Sullivan and Young 1995).

In the south-west a number of turf-walled houses have been excavated on Dartmoor. At Hound Tor and Hutholes small houses with turf walls and sunken floors were found beneath later longhouse settlements. The walls were up to 1.5m thick and had been faced with wattles. The roofs were turf beneath wattle and thatch. The houses had opposed doorways and central hearths, but there was no indication of stalling for animals. They may have been occupied by herdsmen or women who grazed their stock on the open moorland pastures during the summer. Such structures would probably have a life span of 25-30 years on Dartmoor (Beresford 1979).

At Mawgan Porth the houses were built by stripping the hillside of its turf (which could then be used for roofing) and then terracing the house platforms into the hill to provide level foundations. On the uphill side of the site some of the rock was left upstanding to provide a base for the walls, which were on average 0.75m thick. The walls were built of facing stone with a rubble core, without mortar, although clay may have been used as a bonding material. The roofs were supported by timber uprights set in post-holes. The buildings were arranged around four sides of an open courtyard, with their doors opening off it. The principal buildings were of a shortened longhouse type, with both byre and living quarters under the same roof separated by a timber partition. The byre section had a drain in the floor. In Courtyard House 1 the living area was furnished with box beds set in the corners either side of the door, with further beds or benches along the walls. There was a hearth pit with four small stake-holes, possibly for an iron pot-support. The courtyard also had a roofed recess, possibly a dog kennel (Bruce-Mitford 1997).

In conclusion, it is difficult to recognise anything specifically Viking about the Viking Age buildings of England. In general the Scandinavian incomers appear to have adopted native building styles, as there was no reason for them to import their own, although the peculiar class of bow-sided halls might have been a result of Scandinavian influence. Rather the social and economic changes of the Viking Age led to rapid developments in building technology, with the introduction of new foundation methods, such as sill-beams, and new types of structure, such as cellared buildings.

6

FEEDING THE PEOPLE

It has been estimated that the population of England may have doubled between the time of Ælfred and the Domesday Book, increasing from less than one million to almost two million. At the same time a larger proportion of people became less self-sufficient, with increasing numbers living and working in towns. Substantial agricultural expansion would have been necessary to support these changes.

Evidence from throughout England shows that during the Viking Age there was a massive increase in the area farmed, with marginal land being taken under cultivation. These changes were aided by improved climatic conditions in the late ninth and tenth centuries, with shorter milder winters, and longer warmer summers. The Cambridgeshire Fens were first farmed in the tenth and eleventh centuries, and in Warwickshire there was clearance of woodland from marginal land which in many cases had lain deserted since the Roman period. Both the Peak District and the Yorkshire Dales were re-colonised with upland farms such

as Ribblehead (see chapter 3), and there is pollen evidence
for vigorous clearance on Fellend Moss and Steng Moss in
the mid- and late tenth century. On Dartmoor farming was
being undertaken at sites such as Holne Moor; at Gwithian
a heavy plough capable of turning a furrow was in use by
the tenth century (Fowler 1976; 1981).

The lowland zone continued to be intensively farmed.
The area around York, for instance, was already extensively
deforested and had become largely agricultural by the start of
the Viking Age, with a mixture of arable and pastureland and
areas of woodland, some exploited for timber or as coppice
for wattle hurdles and fences. Areas of woodland and marsh,
some quite close to the town, may have been used primarily
for hunting.

The degree to which new farming practices were introduced by Scandinavian settlers remains uncertain. The
origins of the open field system of agriculture is a complex
question, and one to which there may be no single answer
for the whole country. It was certainly in use by the twelfth
century, but may have been introduced in the Anglo-Saxon
or Viking Age, or after the Norman Conquest. It has been
argued that the medieval open field system was introduced
in parts of eastern England in the ninth and tenth centuries.
As we have seen (see chapter 3), this was the period in
which great estates were being broken up over much of the
country, new settlements were being formed, and village
tenements were being laid out, although the Vikings were
just part of this process.

PLANTS AND CEREALS

The four main cereals grown over much of Viking Age England appear to have been wheat, barley, oats and rye. Wheat was grown for flour for bread, barley for brewing, and oats may have been used for animal fodder, as well as porridge. There were some changes from the Roman period in species grown, with the more primitive spelt wheat being less popular. Various legumes, and flax and hemp were also cultivated. In York there are also a number of species likely to have been exploited as herbs or spices, including coriander, dill, opium poppy, and summer savoury. Apples, sloes, plums, cherries, bilberries, blackberries and raspberries were the main fruits consumed; a ninth-century pit from Gloucester full of a residue of apple pips from cider-making suggests that apples were not only eaten. Hazelnuts and walnuts were also consumed; linseed and hempseed were probably used for oil. In York the presence of large quantities of bees suggests that beeswax and honey were both available. In London figs and grapes were imported in small quantities, although hops, presumably brought in for brewing, were relatively abundant.

Most houses, even in towns, seem to have had a quern stone with which to grind their own grain to make bread. The degree of tooth wear common in the period suggests that this was fairly coarse! There is no evidence for windmills before the twelfth century, but earlier watermills have been excavated at Old Windsor and Tamworth. At Old Windsor (Berkshire), there was a large and sophisticated watermill with three vertical wheels by the early ninth century, although this could have been built much earlier. Traces of a stone building with glazed windows and a tiled roof nearby may represent the remains of the royal manor. The mill was totally destroyed by fire in the late ninth or early tenth century. The site was devastated and the mill leat filled in; a second mill with a smaller leat and a horizontal wheel was constructed later in the tenth century, and continued in use until the early eleventh. At Tamworth (Staffordshire) a horizontal-wheeled mill was constructed in the mid-ninth century or earlier, just outside the south-east corner of the *burh* defences, where it could draw water from the river Anker. It was rebuilt in the mid- to late ninth century, with a millpool at a higher level, fed by a reconstructed new leat. Millstones of local and imported stone have been found, as well as grain impressions of oats and possibly barley. Such mills would have been used to process the rents of royal and manorial estates. The second mill at Tamworth was also destroyed by fire, and although it is tempting to attribute the burning down of Old Windsor and Tamworth to Viking raiders, mills often caught fire for more prosaic reasons, notably the heat generated by the milling process itself (Rahtz and Meeson 1992).

ANIMALS

It is unlikely that the Vikings had much effect upon animal husbandry. There is nothing particularly Scandinavian about the bone assemblage at Coppergate, for example, and nothing to suggest the introduction of Scandinavian stock. Nevertheless, there were developments in animal husbandry during the Viking Age in response to general economic trends, and changes, in particular, in the relative importance of various farm animals (Clutton-Brock 1976).

Cattle

Cattle bones are predominant on all Viking Age sites, within and outside the Danelaw, and beef and dairy products would have been the dietary mainstays throughout England. A particularly high proportion of cattle bones has been observed in excavated Viking settlements, namely York, Dublin and Lincoln. We know that the keeping of cattle was culturally important to Viking settlers, and immigrants in Greenland and Iceland stubbornly hung on to their cattle herds, despite the climatic and environmental difficulties. Nevertheless, variations in stock-breeding strategies in England are more likely to have been dictated by local agricultural and economic circumstances than by ethnic affiliations.

Cattle provided most meat in the diet at sites as far apart as Mawgan Porth, Portchester, Cheddar, North Elmham and York. At Flaxengate it has been calculated that cattle provided over 75 per cent of the meat diet. At Coppergate cattle appear to have been brought in on the hoof as required and slaughtered on site, whereas in Durham and Cheddar meat was obtained ready-butchered.

In York the cattle were killed by a blow to the head and butchered in a clumsy and unsystematic fashion which is inconsistent with specialist butchers, in contrast to the Roman period. Evidence from Lincoln suggests that the carcasses were butchered on the floor; they were only hung from timber beams from the eleventh century onwards. There was no careful selection of cattle of a particular age; most were youngish adults, suggesting that cattle had a multi-purpose role as milk producers and draught animals as well as sources of meat. On rural sites oxen would also have been important for pulling the heavy plough.

Sheep and goats

Sheep farming was England's major industry during the Viking Age, but sheep were kept mainly as a source of wool and only secondarily for their meat. Woollen cloth had been a major export from early times. A famous letter of complaint from Charlemagne to Offa of 796 mentions the import of woollen cloaks to France: 'Our people make a demand about the size of the cloaks, that you may order them to be such as used to come to us in former times.'

At North Elmham more sheep bones were found than anything else, but most were from mature animals, indicating that they were being kept for their wool. At Portchester there was a steady increase in the importance of sheep throughout the Saxon period, with animals also being kept until they were older. During the tenth-century sheep coming to slaughter at Flaxengate were drawn from stock being kept for their milk and wool, but during the eleventh century younger animals being bred for their meat were slaughtered.

In York sheep were mainly selected for slaughter between the ages of 18 months and 4 years. In other words, some were being killed after one year's woolclip whilst others were kept for breeding. There is a similar range of fleeces from London and York. Most are from sheep of fairly primitive character with 'hairy' or 'hairy medium' fleeces. There is a higher proportion of 'hairy' sheep in the Viking Age than in Roman Britain and earlier Anglo-Saxon England, but it is not clear that these were introduced by the Vikings, as they are not limited to the Scandinavian area of influence. Nevertheless, in London there was a lower percentage of 'hairy' sheep in the tenth and eleventh centuries than in York, where the proportion was closer to that observed on Norse sites in Scotland.

Viking Age sheep mainly had white fleeces, although the wool was frequently dyed.

In Lincoln there was a marked increase in the proportion of sheep after the mid-tenth century, and a corresponding decline in the number of cattle. This change was not observed in York, where the percentage of sheep is generally lower. The Vale of York is a flat, low-lying area subject to flooding, whereas Lincoln is on a limestone escarpment with rolling chalk hills a few miles to east. Thus the Vale would have been good cattle country in the Viking Age, with sheep being important on the thinner drier chalk and limestone soils of the Wolds, 20km (12 miles) from the city. Sheep would have been important in the more immediate hinterland of Lincoln, and the development of settlement in the Wolds in the Viking Age (see chapter 3) may reflect the growing significance of sheep farming. On the assumption that there were some 4000 adults in Lincoln, O'Connor (1982) calculates that flocks totalling 5000 sheep would be needed to supply the amount of mutton consumed, and that these required between 5000 and 10,000 of acres of grazing. This was a considerable area of farmland to produce only 7 per cent of the meat supply.

Small numbers of goats were also kept in the York area, but formed a minor part of the diet and were principally bred for dairying. The lack of goat bones at Coppergate implies that dairy production was not carried out on a house-by-house basis, but rather that a few suppliers traded milk and cheese in quantity (O'Connor 1989).

Pigs
Viking Age pigs were small dark-skinned hairy beasts with relatively long legs. They were the only animals which could

be kept in towns, and so played a significant part in the urban diet. They were well suited to being fattened and bred in wattle pens in the backyards of urban tenements, although households probably often obtained a pregnant sow from rural farmers. At Coppergate there was a relative increase in the number of pig bones through the Viking Age, and a corresponding decline in cattle bones. At Flaxengate the proportion of pig is fairly constant throughout, unlike cattle and sheep which fluctuate in the tenth century. In Durham it has been suggested that the town residents allowed their pigs to forage in nearby woodland. In the countryside huge herds of pigs may have roamed free-range. In a ninth-century will Ealdorman Ælfred of Surrey bequeathed 2000 pigs to his wife. At Portchester, pigs provided 20 per cent of the diet.

Horses and other animals

Horses were considered to be particularly valuable animals during the Viking Age. They provided only an occasional minor part of diet (at Portchester less than 2 per cent), but were a high-status means of transport and warfare, as attested by the number of spurs and harness fittings from graves and other ritual deposits (see chapter 10).

Deer may have been more important as a source of antler than as potential meat. In York most was collected as shed antler over the winter months. At aristocratic sites with access to hunting forests, such as Portchester, or isolated sites with local wild herds, such as Ribblehead, venison provided an occasional part of the diet.

Cats appear to have been tolerated, but were not looked after as pets. Cat skins were routinely collected. At Thetford the remains of some 18 cats and kittens were found in one pit. Dogs were more abundant and better looked after; at Coppergate, Flaxengate and Thetford there was little evidence for disease or injury on any dog bones. In Lincoln and York they ranged in size from those smaller than a fox to those as big as a wolf, and may have been kept as pets, as guard dogs or for hunting. British hunting dogs were famous and frequently presented as diplomatic gifts in the Viking Age. William of Malmesbury's description of the Welsh tribute to Æthelstan included as many dogs as the king chose 'which could discover with their keen scent the dens and lurking places of wild beasts'. At Thetford all the dogs were of the hound type with relatively long muzzles, and most were the size of a present-day retriever. Some may also have been used as shepherd dogs. At Portchester the absence of dog bones in the domestic refuse has led to the suggestion that the dogs were so highly regarded that they were buried separately.

In towns game animals were relatively rare, but on rural sites such as Ribblehead foxes and hares may have provided a significant supplement to the diet. Certainly the workshops and domestic buildings of the urban centres provided homes for house mice, whilst rats exploited the fringes of the settlements.

Birds

Geese, ducks and chickens were important in both town and country, and were kept around the houses for both meat and eggs. During the tenth century there was a distinct increase in backyard geese and fowl at Coppergate. At Portchester the remains of over 80 chickens and 30 geese were excavated, but the chickens appear to have been kept largely for their eggs. At Cheddar a circular structure with two attached rectangular huts has been interpreted as the remains of a fowl-house with nesting boxes and roosting places in the circular building, with a fowl keeper's dwelling and food store attached.

Game birds are also found in rural and urban deposits, although in York wild birds were never a significant component of the diet, except in so far as they contributed variety. From the late tenth to the early eleventh centuries an increasing diversity of birds was brought to Coppergate. They were mainly wetland species, with some woodland birds, such as wood pigeon and woodcock, moorland birds, including golden plover and black grouse, and cliff-nesting coastal birds, such as guillemot and razor bill. The latter must have been brought from at least 50km (30 miles) away.

At Portchester the remains of numerous wading birds, including golden plover, dunlin, redshank, curlew and woodcock, must represent extensive exploitation of the mud flats. Game birds were considered part of the lordly diet; the remains of 11 curlew in one pit may indicate the leftovers from just one feast. The proportion of birds, particularly ducks, in the York Minster assemblage may reflect the higher status of the site compared to Coppergate.

Marine resources

Clearly seafood was particularly important at coastal settlements such as Mawgan Porth, Green Shiel, and Sandtun (Kent). On Lindisfarne finds included whale and seal; they may have been hunted, but are more likely to represent the exploitation of chance strandings on a nearby beach. Coppergate produced a comb and a sword pommel made from whale bone. The fisherman in Ælfric's *Colloquy*, written in the late tenth century, reports that he caught porpoises and sturgeon, among other fish, but that he declines to catch whales on the grounds that they are too dangerous and may sink the boats sent to hunt them (Gardiner 1997).

Freshwater fish were certainly exploited. At Colwick near Nottingham traces of a Viking Age fishing weir have been discovered (Salisbury 1980). In York the freshwater species included pike, roach, rudd, bream and perch, and especially eels, which could be obtained within or near the town. Fish-hooks from Coppergate and Billingsgate suggest that the inhabitants caught many of their own fish, using a long line. In both London and York, however, there is a common pattern in the early eleventh century with a shift away from the local river resources in favour of the sea. This may be linked to the increased pollution of the rivers as the urban centres expanded. In York there is a decrease in the proportion of salmon, and an increase in cod, with herring, haddock, flat-fish, ling and mackerel also being caught. In Lincoln, cod, haddock and flatfish were being brought in from the coast. In Northampton, herring were imported from the coast.

Shellfish were also widely eaten. In York, oysters were eaten in substantial quantities, and cockles, mussels, and winkles were gathered in smaller proportions. In one particular case a Coppergate pit contained about 2000 mussel shells, along with incidental mussel-bed species, strongly suggesting that this represented the spoiled but unsorted catch of York-based fishermen who had been exploiting mussel beds in the Humber estuary. At Thetford mussels, cockles, winkles and whelks were eaten, and oysters, winkles and mussels at Lindisfarne. The inhabitants of Mawgan Porth ate mussels and snails, keeping them unopened in water tanks constructed of slate slabs.

In summary, the inhabitants of Viking Age England enjoyed a varied diet, with differences in emphasis according to what was available locally. Unsurprisingly there was more variety on rural sites, but 'exotic' foods were also brought to the Viking towns from some distance. The Viking settlement led to no major changes in the animals kept or crops grown, but as the population expanded so agriculture was forced to intensify. The trend visible at Coppergate, but probably also present at other urban sites, indicates a transition from a relatively narrow resource base in the late ninth century, moving through a period in the mid-tenth century in which home-production and the exploitation of local resources was important, to a pattern of commercial trade and exploitation by the late tenth and early eleventh century. By this stage the urban catchment area extended over a wide area, in a manner familiar from later medieval York (O'Connor 1994). The eighth-century *wic* at Fishergate appears to have had limited access to York's environs, and the inhabitants' diet was largely limited to the staple meat species, presumably supplied under the control of the ruling elite. The inhabitants of Coppergate, by contrast, had access to produce of local woods and rivers, in the form of plants and berries, wild game, and marine resources. They were also able to keep a few birds and pigs in their own backyards. This suggests that the Viking Age merchants and craftworkers were able to buy, barter or just go out and collect for themselves items that their more controlled predecessors were denied access to. Whilst there was no immediate change in the ninth century the Viking takeover of York appears to have created a social revolution which laid the foundations for the later medieval period. In York's hinterland the farmers of the East Riding may also have begun to break out of the subsistence cycle, in which the elite consumed the agricultural surplus, with little market penetration other than via the households of the aristocracy. In the same way that the traders of York were now free to range more widely in search of more interesting additions to their diet, so the inhabitants of Cottam may have been freed from royal control and allegiance to the *vill* of Driffield and were now able to sell their produce in the blossoming towns.

7

CRAFT AND INDUSTRY

During the Viking Age the manufacture of basic items such as pottery and iron tools underwent such dramatic changes that it is possible to talk of a 'first Industrial Revolution' (Hodges 1989). Industrial production on any scale had disappeared in England before the end of the Roman occupation, although specialised rural crafts had survived under the patronage of kings and later of the Church. Items of fine jewellery circulated as gifts and tribute, rather than being bought and sold in the market-place. Palace sites such as Cheddar also served as centres for craft specialists working in precious metals. Manorial sites often maintained control of rural resources, with weaving at Goltho, gold and silver-working at Faccombe Netherton, and mass-produced bone tools at Portchester. As urban markets developed, however, they drew craftsmen to them, and acted as centres for the exchange not only of products, but also of ideas. From the early ninth century there were experiments in methods of manufacture, and a trend towards greater standardization which allowed increased productivity. From the late ninth to early tenth century industrial production was revived across a wide range of crafts.

POTTERY

Pottery is a very durable artefact and will always survive wherever it is used. The development of the pottery industry during the Viking Age provides a useful index to the process of industrialisation.

In the early ninth century, no pottery was used over much of the West Midlands and south-west England. In other areas, including Lincoln, York and London, crude pottery was manufactured locally by hand, without the use of a fast wheel, and fired on a bonfire. Only at Ipswich in East Anglia was kiln-fired pottery produced on an industrial scale and traded both overland and along the coast from Yorkshire to Kent (Hurst 1976).

From the middle decades of the ninth century changes begin to occur at a number of centres. These developments cannot be attributed to Scandinavian settlers as they were underway before their arrival, but the adoption of industrialised wheelthrown production certainly corresponds to those areas of Mercia and the Danelaw which underwent military reorganisation (Mellor 1980; Vince 1985; 1991). They may be associated with increased marketing opportunities developing in the ninth century towns. In late ninth-century York there were the first steps towards a specialised industry with handmade wares now produced in standardised forms and fabrics (Mainman 1990). In East Anglia the Ipswich potters began to use a wheel to make cooking pots in a sandy fabric on a large scale in what is known as the Thetford tradition.

By 900 wheel-thrown pottery was manufactured over much of eastern England. The manufacture of Thetford-type wares soon spread to other East Anglian towns, and tenth-century kilns have been excavated in Pottergate, Norwich and in Thetford itself. York was producing wheel-thrown pottery by the beginning of the tenth century, and Lincoln by the mid-tenth century. In York, wheel-thrown pottery fired at a high temperature developed from the local handmade types. The simple York ware cooking pots could be produced easily by local potters unfamiliar with the wheel, and are the principal domestic ware found at Coppergate throughout the late ninth and early tenth centuries. In the East Midlands, the handmade shelly wares at sites such as Eaton Socon developed into the wheel-thrown St Neots ware. In Wessex industrial pottery production evolved more slowly out of the local handmade tradition. The first results were fairly crude and often finished by hand, but by the mid-tenth century, respectable wheel-thrown pots were being fired in single-flue kilns. The range of forms also increased, with bowls, dishes, lamps and pitchers all being thrown.

South of the Thames and in the north-west, production continued on a small scale with handmade pots fired on a bonfire continuing as the main products well into the tenth century, alongside wheel-thrown forms. Crude handmade pottery reached Cornwall in the ninth century, and continued in use well into the eleventh century. Squat cooking vessels with flat grass-marked bases and distinctive bar-lug handles form most of the assemblage at Gwithian and Mawgan Porth. The style is also found throughout the western Baltic and north Germany and was once thought to be Viking; it has since been suggested that it was introduced by Frisian traders.

By 950 industrial-scale wheel-thrown production had supplanted handmade wares at over 30 centres. This new pottery production was notably town-based: Northampton, Stamford, Stafford, Thetford and Winchester are all examples of new wares which take their names from the towns in which kilns have been discovered. Kilns have been excavated in four of the five Scandinavian boroughs; and their absence at Derby is probably due to the lack of excavation. Stafford ware, or Chester-type ware, as it is sometimes known, was produced at the Tipping Street kilns in Stafford in a Thetford ware tradition from the mid-tenth century, and soon spread throughout the Mercian *burhs*.

Urban potters may have had difficulty acquiring enough fuel, and for this reason, and because of the risk of fire, many kilns may still have been situated on the edges of towns. The St Neots ware potters still fired their vessels to a fairly low temperature on an open bonfire; elsewhere the single-flue kiln was now widely used. Production normally involved the use of local clays. The reputation of Stamford ware was based upon local estuarine clays found on the Fen margins which did not require additives. At Torksey, where Frankish potters brought by the Danes after their overwintering in 872 began producing a distinctive type of pottery, the fabric was rougher because of the presence of sandy quartz crystals in the local clay. For St Neots ware the clay was tempered with crushed shells.

Decoration might be added to vessels by thumbing, incising, combing, stabbing or rouletting, or by the addition of strips or stamped motifs. Glazing was relatively uncommon and was probably restricted to high-quality luxury items; a number of production sites have now been identified, but the similarities between them suggest that the potters had a common source for their techniques. It may be significant that many of the early glazed-ware production centres are also known for glass manufacture. The potters generally selected white-firing clays, enabling them to achieve a clear yellow or olive-green colour. Experiments in glazing dark reduced wares, such as at Lincoln, tended to be short-lived. Glazed pottery was generally produced according to a restricted range of forms, including spouted pitchers, lamps, and sprinklers.

The most famous pre-Conquest glazed pottery form in England is the spouted pitcher with a pale yellow, orange or green glaze produced from a fine off-white clay at Stamford, and traded throughout England (Kilmurry 1980). The start of pottery production in Stamford coincides with the Scandinavian occupation in the mid-ninth century. As the settlement developed into a town so the pottery production and trade grew. The Stamford potters specialised in four main types of pottery: cooking vessels (small pots and bowls), table wares (for food and drink), lamps, and crucibles. The distribution of their kilns suggests that there were several individual workshops, lying outside the town walls.

The crucibles and fine tableware, pitchers and jugs were exported far afield, but the bulk of Stamford production was of cooking pots which were distributed locally in south Lincolnshire. The Stamford industry may be characterised as a basic industry sustained by a local market which was growing at a rate rapid enough to support an upsurge in production and a shift to an industrial base. Glaze and red paint were used in Stamford from the beginning, in the late ninth century. Their sudden appearance suggests that they may have been introduced by foreign potters working in Stamford. These are unlikely to have been Danes, as the idea originated in northern France or the Low Countries. Nevertheless, its origin should be seen in the context of Viking disruption in north-west Europe, and the potters may have arrived 'in the Viking baggage train'. With the interaction between Denmark and England during Knutr's reign, and the consequent free movement of craftsmen, the glazed Stamford ware tradition spread back to Scandinavia.

Experiments with glazing local Lincoln wares in the late ninth century may also be seen as Viking-influenced, but the pottery was unsuitable and the attempts were short-lived (Gilmour 1988). In York there is little evidence for experimentation in glazes on local wares. The Early Glazed wares, which have now been identified in tenth-century levels, are all well produced and hard-fired. They are all of a very small size and may possibly have served some specialist function such as containers for oils or perfumes. The similar development of tenth-century glazed wares at Northampton, Winchester, Portchester and Michelmersh can all be seen as inspired by Stamford, or derived from the same continental origin.

CARPENTRY

The relative abundance of pottery on most sites can lead archaeologists to exaggerate its importance. Other materials which are not found as often may have been just as common at the time. Wood, for example, may have been preferred for plates, bowls and cups; and wooden barrels may have been used for storage and transport. Wooden objects may have been lavishly decorated but rarely survive, a saddle-bow from Coppergate being a rare exception. Where wood survives it is often abundant; at the Saddler Street site, Durham, six wooden vessels were recovered compared with 30 pottery ones.

Timber was used selectively, with a view to the properties of different woods. Evidence from London indicates that a variety of tree-producing land must have existed in south-east England. There must have been large areas of coppiced woodland which was harvested for wattlework, but also large oaks, sometimes up to 1m in diameter, growing in remnants of ancient forest or in former Roman managed plantations (Milne 1992). At Coppergate the post-and-wattle structures were predominantly of oak, hazel and willow, whilst oak provided the massive timbers used in the later cellared buildings. Lathe turning was being carried out nearby, as there were large numbers of waste cores; many had been dumped in an abandoned building. Lathe-turned bowls and cups of maple, alder and ash were found (*plate 8*); indeed, the derivation of the name Coppergate is thought to be 'the street of the cup-makers' (Hall 1994). Specialist wood-working tools, including adzes, axes, augers and boring bits, chisels and draw knives have been found on both rural and urban sites and in metalworker's hoards of scrap iron. The saw, however, was not known until after the Norman Conquest.

BONE, ANTLER, IVORY AND HORN WORKING

Large-scale antler and bone working, and to a lesser extent horn working, seems to be characteristic of Viking Age towns, although it is unclear whether it should be regarded as a craft or an industry (MacGregor 1985). Many of the simple types of object could have been made by anyone, although the more sophisticated combs were probably made by specialists (*plate 30*). Analysis of the evidence from Sweden concludes that combs were made exclusively by itinerant workers who travelled from one market to another. Antler and bone working certainly seems to have been widespread and evidence has been recovered from Chester, Ipswich, Lincoln, Northampton, Oxford and several York sites, including Coppergate, and York Minster. The distribution of offcuts and waste at Coppergate suggests that there may have been foci of activity in one or two of the buildings at different periods of the site's history. There is insufficient debris, however, to suggest a long-term settled workshop and it has been suggested that itinerant craftsmen operated from these tenements. Significantly these craftsmen were able to adapt to changing fashions, producing objects decorated in both Anglo-Saxon and Anglo-Scandinavian art styles (MacGregor *et al.* 1999).

In Viking Age towns animal bones would have been readily available as domestic waste, although particular bones were deliberately selected for each product. Bone was used occasionally for combs, but also for pins, textile equipment, playing pieces, toggles and skates. Antler was favoured for comb making, but was also used for knife handles. In both Lincoln and York the antler was mostly from shed antlers which must have been collected in the surrounding woods, although there is rather more evidence for the hunting of deer from Lincoln (Mann 1982). Walrus ivory was also worked to produce fine mounts and fittings; elephant ivory is rare in Viking Age England, although two fragments are known from York.

STONE

Before the tenth century the development of stone quarrying for building and stone sculpture was largely in response to demand from the church. At Raunds the site of a Viking Age quarry has been identified as the source of materials for the new stone church. The quarries around Lincoln were producing stone for grave covers and also for the first generation of stone-built churches in the city. Good building stone was also quarried at sites such as Portland and the Isle of Wight, and transported over long distances of more than 80km (50 miles), for the construction of the new stone churches (Jope 1964). In Lincolnshire it is clear from the distribution of the sculpture that waterways were used to transport these large and heavy objects. Particular types of stone were sometimes selected for certain features, such as Barnack limestone for the alternate long and short ashlar blocks at the corners of church towers. Where they were available, however, Roman buildings were robbed for their dressed ashlar blocks, such as those reused in the tower of St Mary Bishophill Junior, in York. Roman stone was also exported to York's hinterland, for use in both monuments and churches. The arches still standing in the church at Kirk

Hammerton, 13.5km (8 miles) north-west of York, may have been demolished from a substantial Roman building and carefully reconstructed, piece by piece. In Yorkshire crosses and grave slabs were generally made from a single piece of local stone which was rarely transported more than 15km (*c.*10 miles).

In the tenth century the Scandinavian aristocracy took over the patronage of the stone masons and sculptors. Large quantities of crosses and tombstones were produced for this new market (see chapter 11). Sculptural workshops were established in towns, such as Chester and York (*plate 9*), or around rural sites, such as Gosforth (Cumbria). In York a group of carvers, which have been collectively termed the 'Metropolitan School' virtually mass produced a standard range of monuments which are found in graveyards across the city. These craftsmen inherited much of their artistic reper-toire from the Anglo-Saxon church to which they added Viking Age animal ornament (see chapter 11).

The sculptor's first task would be to give the monument its basic shape. Analysis demonstrates that templates were regularly used, to produce the shape of a cross-head for instance. The decoration would then be laid out in panels; templates and stencils were again used to produce elements of the design. Different workshops produced monuments with distinctive styles and designs. Similarities between groups of sculpture show that itinerant masons travelled between villages. It has been argued that the same template was used to provide the outline of a warrior's helmet on a cross at Sockburn (Durham) as at Brompton (North Yorkshire), some 11km (7 miles) away, implying that the industry was carefully controlled. Chisels and punches would be used to carve the stone, which would then be decorated with bright colours. The scrubbed appearance of stone sculpture today makes it difficult to envisage the original intended appearance, which to a modern eye would have been exceptionally gaudy. Gesso, a form of plaster, was sometimes used as a base, and then black, blue, red, brown, orange, yellow and white paints would be used to highlight the design. Finally, the sculptor may have added decorative metalwork, jewellery or paste.

GLASS

Glass was used for tableware, mainly fine cups and beakers for wine consumption, and occasionally for glazing windows, where its use was restricted to stone buildings. Fragments of window glass have been found at monastic sites, such as Jarrow, Monkwearmouth and Repton, and at aristocratic sites, such as the royal manor at Old Windsor. Glass was made with soda-lime until the tenth century, when the increased demand for window glass was met by the use of potash. With the possible exception of Barking Abbey, none of the excavated sites where glazing occurs has so far yielded furnace remains, one possibility being that ready-made glass was brought to the site for cutting. Glass beads and other jewellery was manufactured in towns, and glass-smelting crucibles have been found in Gloucester, Lincoln and York. At Winchester a pit excavated at the Brooks site contained a large collection of predominantly window glass, presumably brought together for recycling (Hunter and Heyworth 1998). At Coppergate a glassworking hearth may have been in operation in the late ninth century, even before the tenements were established. A group of 29 fragments, predominantly of Roman glass vessels, had been collected nearby, presumably for melting down. By the later Viking Age lead was being added to the crucibles to give the glass a sparkling appearance, like modern lead crystal. Beads, finger rings, and playing pieces were manufactured from the yellow and dark green glasses (Hall 1994).

NON-FERROUS METALWORKING

The working of copper alloys and precious metals was restricted to aristocratic sites for much of the post-Roman period, and appears to have been carried out under lordly or ecclesiastical patronage. A mould fragment from Whitby Abbey is more likely to represent monastic metalworking than Viking raiders pausing from pillage to melt down church plate. At Cheddar, gold, copper, silver, tin and lead were worked in the ninth century. Jewellery was the main product, possibly for gifts from the king to his retinue. At Faccombe Netherton, on a site adjacent to the aisled hall, copper alloys and gold were cast in the tenth century. Such communities of craftworkers must have been established at many rural manorial sites.

During the Viking Age non-ferrous metalworking also becomes an urban enterprise, and evidence has been found in several towns, including Chester, Exeter, Lincoln, Northampton, Thetford and York. At Coppergate two adjacent tenth-century tenements were occupied by metal-workers. Each had a large central hearth which may have been used for heating metals, and some 1000 crucible fragments were found, of which over 90 per cent were of Stamford ware. The smallest, no larger than a thimble, appear to have been used for melting gold, but silver, lead and copper alloys were also being worked. There is no direct evidence for the smelting of non-ferrous metals, though pieces of galena (lead ore) show that it was being brought to the city. The metalworkers were separating precious from base metals in small ceramic dishes. Contemporary finds of coin dies and trial stamps (see chapter 8) suggest that much of the silver may have been used for coinage but the main trade appears to have been jewellery production, and several unfinished objects were excavated. Any suitable material might be utilised as a mould; a Roman tile had shapes cut into it for casting blanks for brooches and pendants. Both stone and clay moulds were used for casting ingots, but soapstone moulds were selected for silver casting. Soapstone is found in Shetland, Norway, France and Sweden. Its use in York, the only site in England where it fulfils this purpose, suggests that it was brought from Shetland or Scandinavia by Scandinavian traders or craftsmen. Silver ingots would be used as the raw material for further casting, or might be hammered into arm rings. One of the most remarkable aspects of the Coppergate finds is the range of metalworking activities represented, often concentrated in the same areas, perhaps indicating sharing of workshop facilities (Bayley 1992).

At Flaxengate, Lincoln, a similar range of metals was worked in the same buildings as glass beads were being made, although silver and copper alloys decline in importance in the late tenth century, to be replaced by iron-working. Over 500 crucible fragments have been excavated from ninth- to eleventh-century levels. The crucibles were manufactured from local clays or, if they were to be used for melting silver, crucibles imported from Stamford were preferred.

During the ninth and tenth centuries the demand for brooches decorated in a Scandinavian style spread beyond those who could afford precious metals. Iron alloys and pewter became particularly popular for mass-produced jewellery (*plates 11 and 31*). A large number of lead alloy disc brooches appear to have been manufactured on Coppergate. They were decorated with stylised animals and plants and geometric motifs. Scandinavian Jellinge, Borre and Ringerike style elements were each manufactured in England. Designs might first be tested on 'trial' or 'motif-pieces' of waste bone (*plate 13*).

Recording of objects found by metal detector users has revealed large numbers of Anglo-Scandinavian-style objects in the hinterlands of the Viking Age towns (Thomas 2000). In Lindsey, for example, over 200 objects have been recorded, the vast majority being poor quality jewellery (Leahy pers comm). Many of the items are also very worn, presumably because they were everyday costume fittings. Metal detecting has also brought to light Viking objects from all over Norfolk and Suffolk (Margeson 1997). Some were made in Scandinavia; others were made locally in a Scandinavian style. Sometimes new types of artefact were created that are neither Scandinavian nor Anglo-Saxon, but represent a new cultural identity (MacGregor 1982; Tweddle 1986). The flat disc brooches so beloved of the Anglo-Saxons, now decorated with Scandinavian ornament, are a sure sign of mixed traditions. So-called Norse bells are not known from Scandinavia, but are found in Scandinavian colonies overseas from Iceland to Yorkshire. Two have been found at the Anglo-Scandinavian settlement at Cottam (*plate 32*); their function is unknown but they were probably decorative costume fittings. Williams (1997) has catalogued over 500 stirrup-strap mounts: decorative mounts with elements of Ringerike or Urnes style ornament, which were attached to iron stirrups. These objects have been discovered throughout lowland England but were probably in use for a relatively short period of time, between 1025-1100. Could these represent a short-lived fashion, possibly of an elite cavalry group with Scandinavian pretensions?

IRON WORKING

Iron was probably the most important raw material during the Viking Age, being essential for both tools and weapons. The blacksmith enjoyed particular prestige, and appears in Scandinavian mythological scenes depicted on stone monuments as a heroic figure, such as Weland the Smith who was lamed by the king to prevent him from escaping with his skills, or Regin who forged the magical sword used by Sigurd the dragon-slayer. A tenth-century cross from Halton (Lancashire), for example, appears to show Regin working at a raised hearth.

In Middle Saxon England there was a relatively restricted range of iron products. There were weapon smiths at a few permanent centres, including rural proto-manors such as Wharram Percy, but most smiths were itinerant or village craftsmen manufacturing and mending tools on a small scale for local consumption. In Viking Age England, iron-smithing became a town industry, and urban excavations invariably provide evidence for iron working. Rural communities, such as those at Ribblehead, St Neots, Thwing, and Wharram Percy, still undertook production for their own needs, and at higher status rural sites such as Cheddar most of the iron objects required would also have been made on site. The key developments, however, took place in towns such as Bedford, Northampton, Stamford, Lincoln and York, where smiths experimented with new artefacts and new techniques.

Iron working is a two-stage process. First the ore must be smelted to extract the iron, and then the iron must be worked by the smith to make finished artefacts. Smelting is a very hot and unpleasant process which requires great quantities of fuel. It is likely that most smelting was still undertaken in the country, close to the iron ore deposits, and abundant supplies of wood, at sites like West Runton, Great Casterton and Ashdown Forest (Sussex). At Ramsbury (Wiltshire) industrial iron furnaces dated to the late eighth and early ninth centuries have been excavated, which most likely operated within the sphere of royal influence (McDonnell 1989).

Scrap iron was a precious commodity and several hoards of broken iron tools and weapons have been found in England, although it is not always possible to distinguish them from ritual river deposits (see chapter 2). In many cases metal-workers' hoards include ancient Roman and Anglo-Saxon objects. At Nazeing (Essex) an eleventh-century hoard found in alluvial gravels on the east side of the river Lea comprised four axes, four spearheads, a gouge, a chisel, a small hammer, a ploughshare, two knives, a fish spear, and a copper alloy ring and cup (Morris 1983). Similar hoards are known from Hurbuck (Co Durham), Crayke (North Yorkshire), and Westley Waterless (Cambridgeshire).

Little smelting was undertaken in towns, other than at Stamford where iron ore was brought from the local ironstone outcrops. In York carbonate ore would have been available from either North Yorkshire or Lincolnshire. At Coppergate some 21kg (46lb) of iron smelting slag has been excavated, including some solidified into the hemispherical shape of the furnace bottoms. Nonetheless this is less than might be expected from a single smithing operation. Excavation of the furnace of Millbrook (Sussex), for example, produced over 40kg of smelting slag. The evidence does not therefore suggest that smelting was undertaken in the immediate vicinity of Coppergate. Much of the slag may have been brought to the site as rubbish, possibly after use as ballast in ships on the Foss. The vast majority of bar iron being used in Anglo-Scandinavian York was probably smelted close to the ore source (Ottaway 1992).

Smithing was far more widespread. It has been identified at Flaxengate in Lincoln, and at the Minster and Coppergate sites in York. In both Lincoln and York there was a close relationship between the ferrous and non-ferrous metalworkers; both sets of activities were often carried on in the same buildings, probably by the same workers. Approximately 179kg (400lb) of smithing slag was excavated at Coppergate. Iron bars and strips were imported from the smelting sites outside York and large amounts of material were also brought for recycling. It is now believed that even the remarkable Coppergate Anglian helmet probably reached the site as scrap.

The Coppergate smiths displayed a high degree of expertise and were probably permanent craftsmen. A number of classes of object were manufactured on site, including needles, jewellery, and Scandinavian-style chest fittings. At the

York Minster site the smiths were mass-producing horseshoe nails in a former Roman barrack block. Different grades of iron were selected for different purposes. Around 220 knives were found in Viking Age deposits at Coppergate. Most made use of carbonised steel for the cutting edge. During the ninth century new types of knife were introduced, including a group with long handles, and decoration proliferated, including incised grooves and inlaid designs (Ottaway 1992). Clearly knives and iron dress-fittings were being increasingly used for decoration and display in the Viking Age. Although it is difficult to identify any particular Scandinavian influence, the increased need for status display may be seen as a reflection of the Viking Age circumstances.

Manufacturing techniques were also developing at the same time, and a great variety of methods were in use by the tenth century. There were two principal methods of welding the steel blade to an iron knife. The hardest knives were produced by butt-welding the steel strip along the edge of the iron blade. Another technique was to sandwich weld a steel blade in between two slices of iron. This second method increased in popularity in York during the tenth century, leading to knives becoming softer. Sandwich-welding was also introduced into Dublin at this time, possibly from York.

LEATHER WORKING

By the medieval period leather working comprised several specialist tasks, such as skinning, tanning, dressing and cobbling, but during the Viking Age these may have been

combined under one roof. Leather working developed on a
professional basis in towns and was carried out as a commercial activity. In Durham the Saddler Street leather workers
obtained uncut oxhide which they made into shoes, boots
and knife-sheaths. They also acted as cobblers, repairing
shoes. In York leather workers made shoes, boots, sword and
knife-sheaths. Hides from cows slaughtered on site would
have provided them with a ready supply of leather, after it
had been tanned. In Chester a large scale eleventh-century
tanning industry was discovered at Lower Bridge Street.

TEXTILES

By the ninth century there was some trade in textiles, but
most communities produced cloth for their own needs.
Large estates would supply their own wool, flax and
dyestuffs, and prepare, spin, weave, and dye their own textiles.
Some estates were apparently able to employ servants and
slaves to work on textile manufacture. At the manorial site
at Goltho, a weaving house has been identified from the
pin-beaters and other textile tools found on the floor of a
large outbuilding.

Urban communities may also have produced homespun
textiles for local demand from raw materials bought in
from the countryside. In York all the processes of production, from taking the raw wool to making it into finished
cloth and garments, were being practised in the first 40 or
50 years of Anglo-Scandinavian occupation of Coppergate.
Although textile working was essentially a home-based
craft, York's international trading contacts would have meant

that any surplus might have reached markets from Ireland to Samarkand. The Coppergate and Flaxengate sites were littered with textile implements, including shears, wool combs, and spindlewhorls (perforated weights made of animal bone, pottery sherds, stone or occasionally lead, which weighted the hand-held spindles on which woollen thread was spun out). At Coppergate wool was probably cleaned within the tenement buildings, in view of the abundant sheep lice. In the ninth century the wool was then woven into lengths of cloth using a warp-weighted loom whereby the warp threads were suspended from the top of loom and weighted by loomweights made of circles of fired clay. By the tenth century the warp-weighted loom was probably no longer used on Coppergate, being replaced by the two-beam vertical loom, whereby the warp threads are attached to a wooden beam (Walton Rogers 1997). In Lincoln and Winchester the comparative rarity of loomweights has led to the suggestion that the two-beam vertical loom was introduced from the Continent in the late ninth century, although the warp-weighted loom may have remained in favour on rural sites. At Goltho the two-beam loom was in use in the tenth century. It has also been suggested that the treadle-operated horizontal loom was in use in Gloucester by the tenth century, although elsewhere it is not known until the eleventh century (Pritchard 1984).

The people of York probably dyed their own textiles as well, and a variety of dye plants such as madder and woad are characteristic of Viking Age deposits. Their clothing was probably a mass of colour, with evidence for reds, greens, blues, yellows and blacks. White linen, woven from vegetable fibres, was probably preferred for undergarments and bedlinen. Smooth glass 'linen-smoothers' used for the finishing of linen cloth have been found in Lincoln, London, Thetford, Winchester and York.

There is very little particularly Scandinavian about the Coppergate textiles, however. The majority of textiles have more in common with those of Anglo-Saxon England and Carolingian Europe than with Scandinavia, and the tools of textile production remain typically Anglo-Saxon (Walton Rogers 1997). There are none of the black clay conical whorls which are common throughout Scandinavia. The Coppergate spindlewhorls are regional types which belong in a local northern Anglo-Saxon tradition; the wool comb can be matched by one from Cottam. Most of the textiles are local products, although there are some fine broken chevron twills, probably imported from Frisia, one of which had been dyed with lichen purple. A group of patterned linens, including a honeycomb weave, may have originated in the Rhineland, and may have been brought to York by Frisian merchants following the wine trade route (Walton 1989). The only clear Viking textile is a tenth-century woollen sock made in a technique known as *nålebinding*, or needle-binding which looks like close-textured crochet work, although this is more likely to have arrived on the foot of its owner, rather than in a batch of imported socks (*plate 12*). A similar example is known from a textile fragment from a Viking burial at Heath Wood, Ingleby (Derbyshire).

Silks are known from a number of Viking Age towns, including York, Lincoln, Dublin and London. These must have been imported, most probably by Scandinavians operating the trade route along the Russian rivers to the silk road. At Coppergate, tabby-weave silks appear to have been cut up and sewn on site, probably for silk head-dresses, possibly in a Scandinavian fashion.

In summary, the origins of industrial production can be observed in many crafts during the Viking Age. The thriving towns of lowland England represented a tremendous commercial opportunity, with a concentration of demand for cheaply-produced metalwork, trinkets and other consumer goods. Within their walls, groups of craftworkers and merchants would act together, or in sequence, on certain materials, forming chains of interlinked crafts. In York we can observe a local, rural Anglo-Saxon textile industry moving into the town in the mid-ninth century and, over the following centuries, taking up new technology as it became available.

The role of Scandinavian settlers and traders in this upsurge in industrial production is not straightforward. In York the introduction of Anglo-Saxon rather than Scandinavian textile tools into the town prompts the evocative suggestion that this traditionally female industry may have remained in the hands of local Anglo-Saxon women, drawn into the town, whilst the impact of Scandinavians was on crafts which were traditionally male, such as metalworking. Some York crafts show production for a number of tastes, with antler and bone objects, for example, being produced in both Anglo-Saxon and Anglo-Scandinavian styles. In other cases we can observe the development of new integrated fashions. In jewellery manufacture Scandinavian-style animal ornament was executed on Anglo-Saxon disc brooches; Scandinavian oval brooches were not made in York.

Some industrialisation was underway before the Scandinavian settlement. The development of the pottery industry, for instance, had already begun in eastern England. Glazing is not restricted to Danelaw sites, and is not found at all of them. Nevertheless, wheel-thrown pottery was introduced into most parts of England during the Viking Age. The potential for increased sales provided the incentive for experimentation in new methods which enabled mass production. The significance of the introduction of the kick wheel, and other innovations such as single-flue kilns and glazing, is that they required capital investment and a full-time commitment to pottery production. This was only worthwhile if there was a large demand and a marketing infrastructure, including markets, a transport system, and a means of exchange.

Urban demand and marketing opportunities increased throughout the late ninth and tenth centuries. Changes in land ownership may have permitted new ways of obtaining raw materials, breaking the ties of Anglo-Saxon society and allowing craftsmen to operate more for personal profit. In the countryside prosperous farmers celebrated their wealth by purchasing Scandinavian-style consumer goods. Although the Vikings may not have started the tenth-century 'Industrial Revolution' they did provide both the stimulus and the mechanism for it to happen.

8

TRADE AND EXCHANGE

In recent years the role of the Vikings in stimulating international trade and peaceful commerce has been emphasised, and
their warlike activities played down (Sawyer 1986). Analysis of
the foreign goods imported into England, however, suggests
that their role as traders, at least initially, may have been exaggerated. Although the variety of exotic goods does reflect
a wide range of long-distance contacts, the proportion of
imported goods in ninth- and tenth-century England is relatively small.

We have already seen that the Vikings disrupted many of
the Saxon trading sites (see chapter 4). In contrast to the
large number of imports from the sixth to ninth centuries,
imported goods are equally rare in tenth-century Ipswich,
Norwich, London, Southampton, Winchester and York.
London was affected by a recession in long-distance trade
during the tenth century. In York only 500 of the 15,000
objects found at Coppergate were imported, and virtually
the only tenth-century imported finds are a silk cap, a

brooch from the Low Countries and a Badorf-type amphora. Significantly, there was not a single piece of Scandinavian pottery in some 55,000 pottery sherds found in Viking Age levels at Coppergate. The lifestyle of the inhabitants of York would not have been noticeably affected if international trading contacts ceased. In Yorkshire, Lincolnshire and East Anglia, local and regional trade was far more important than international trade. On the other hand, the prosperity of tenth-century Chester appears to have rested on its role as the pre-eminent English trading site in the north-west. The production of the Chester mint is likely to reflect the trading activities of private individuals and the transformation of silver bullion into coinage. Chester is the most common mint represented in English coins found in Dublin and its hinterland, and Chester-type ware has also been found in Dublin, as well as in Trondheim. Indeed, whilst sharing few archaeological parallels with York, Chester shares several with Dublin (Ward 1994).

TRADED GOODS

Traded goods can be difficult to recognise from archaeo-logical evidence. The trading of slaves is documented in the sixth and seventh centuries, and continued into Viking Age England. The Vikings were well-attested slavers throughout Europe, although there are no direct archaeological traces in England. Chester may have been an important port for slaves from Dublin and the ringed pins recovered from the town may indicate the presence of Hiberno-Norse traders. From their port of entry slaves may have been sold on throughout

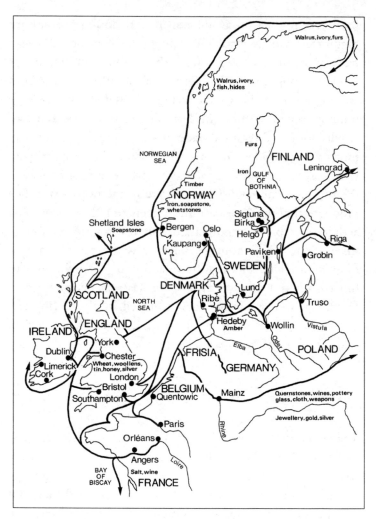

12 Map of Viking Age trade routes in north-west Europe (after Graham-Campbell 1990)

England. During Viking raids it is likely that Anglo-Saxons may have been carried off as slaves, and that was probably the fate of some citizens of Southampton, captured in a raid in 980. The Church did not object to slavery as such and the Domesday Book reveals large scale ownership of slaves on church lands, but it was concerned to prevent slaves being exported overseas, lest they were unable to practise their religion. The slave trade was outlawed in 1102 but slavery was not prohibited (Pelteret 1981).

Organic commodities also leave little trace and even where remains of wool, cloth or grain are preserved it is difficult to distinguish imported from local goods. Nonetheless, on the basis of palaeo-environmental evidence from Coppergate, it is probable that considerable quantities of clubmoss were imported from Scandinavia (Kenward and Hall 1995); its use was presumably as a mordant for dyeing the textiles produced on the sites. On the other hand, only very small quantities of fig and grape indicate imports from warmer climates.

The principal objects which may have been imported to England from Scandinavia for which evidence survives are those of walrus ivory, steatite or soapstone, and schist. In the tenth century a Norwegian ivory trader, Ohthere, visited Ælfred's court, and described his journey from his home in northern Norway to the market places of southern Scandinavia at Hedeby and Kaupang, where he sold or exchanged the Arctic products he had collected. Walrus ivory is known from York and Lincoln, and an implement from Bramham (West Yorkshire) may have been imported through York, before being dispersed into its hinterland. The quantities, however, are very small, and may have been personal possessions of Viking settlers. Similarly, the soapstone bowls from Flaxengate and Coppergate are so worn that they look more like prized personal heirlooms rather than imported goods (*plate 14*). Soapstone was also quarried on Shetland and may have been imported from there in preference to Norway. Amber is more likely to have been collected on the east coast than imported from Denmark. Neither amber nor soapstone have so far been recorded from tenth- or eleventh-century London. Schist honestones, which must have come from southern Norway, are known from several sites with Danelaw links, including York, Lincoln, Northampton, Thetford and London. Even so, the trade may have been directed through the Low Countries in the hands of Frisian traders from Dorestad, rather than being imported direct from Scandinavia. In fact, England's Viking Age imports demonstrate little change from her Middle Saxon trading partners, and continued links with Germany and northern France, although there is apparently a reduction in volume. The most visible items are quernstones and pottery, although it is assumed that the latter was being imported in association with the Rhenish wine trade. The wine was transported in amphorae and narrow barrels, like those depicted in the Bayeaux Tapestry, and which are found reused as well linings in Milk Street, London; but decorated pitchers and beakers were bought to accompany it, so that Rhenish wine might be served from Pingsdorf spouted pitchers and drunk from Pingsdorf beakers. Pingsdorf and Badorf ware has been recognised on some 20 sites, but are rarely found in large quantities. Fewer than 15 imported vessels were discarded on Coppergate in 150 years, in contrast to Anglian York where imported pottery was far more common. The distribution of Rhenish wares is not limited to the Danelaw, although there are a few sherds from Lincoln and Thetford, as well as those from York. Outside the Danelaw, in the south and east, French red-painted wares are more common than Rhenish products.

Imported German Mayen-Niedermendig lava millstones may have followed the same route as the wine trade. Their importation was already well-established in Anglo-Saxon England. In the Viking Age they are known from towns such as Lincoln, Thetford and York, and rural sites such as St Neots and Springfield, although more isolated farmsteads, such as Ribblehead, were using the inferior millstone grit.

The only imported item which perhaps reveals Scandinavian traders acting as middlemen is silk, for which the nearest production centre is in the east Mediterranean. The most likely route by which bales of Byzantine silk might have reached England is up the Russian river systems and then to Scandinavia and on to England. Silk has been identified on the Danelaw sites of York and Lincoln, and in a tenth-century pit from Milk Street, London. Some 23 fragments have been recovered from Coppergate, mostly from the period 930-70. A silk cap shares a distinctive weaving flaw with a fragment from Lincoln, suggesting that it might have been cut from the same bale of material (Walton 1989).

Whilst international trade during the Viking Age appears to have been fairly limited, there was still a vigorous home market. Most goods which were traded internally within England were probably perishable agricultural products, and are almost impossible to identify. The remarkable national trade in pottery, however, gives some indication of the likely scale of trade (*12*). Even rural settlements such as Raunds and Wharram Percy were supplied with a full range of Late Saxon pottery. Some pottery may have been transported as containers and its spread may reflect the commodity trade; the distribution of Thetford ware within and from East Anglia, for example, may represent the movement of grain. Other pottery, such as lead-glazed Stamford ware (see chapter 7), appears to have been regarded as a luxury product in its own right.

The trade in Stamford ware may well have started with specialist industrial pottery; glazed crucibles are the first Stamford ware pottery to appear on tenth-century metal-working sites in Lincoln, Thetford and York. Later, with the production of fine table wares in the same fabric, the trade expanded dramatically and Stamford ware pitchers are found throughout central England. By the eleventh century it accounts for almost 25 per cent of all pottery in Lincoln and York. The proportion of Stamford ware decreases gradually with distance away from the Stamford kilns. There is a central core, a circle with a radius of *c.*24km (15 miles), within which it is most common fabric, although local shelly and limestone wares still continue in use alongside it, and an outer area of up to 80km (50 miles) away where it is consistently present in smaller amounts. The local Stamford ware distribution may reflect local farmers coming to market, but outside its local base the pattern of trade of Stamford ware is a Viking one. Its appearance on virtually every Lincolnshire site implies an organised trade involving middlemen who specialised in the sale of pottery. The trade was maintained along coastal and riverine routes. Transport by water would have been slow but also safe; the rivers Welland and Ouse were navigable and Stamford ware finds cluster along the former line of the Wash and up the Lincolnshire coast, to Whitby and as far afield as Aberdeen and Perth. The trade was not maintained to the same extent southwards; there is no Stamford ware in London before the Norman Conquest for example.

The distribution of other Viking Age pottery, such as Cheddar, Stafford and Late Saxon Shelly wares, is also restricted to certain areas, although our understanding of what such distributions mean is still in its infancy. Some patterns, such as the Thames-valley distribution of the Oxford shelly wares, may reflect distribution by river, but in other cases we may be plotting the areas of influence of various Viking and Anglo-Saxon groups. In Oxford, for example, it has been suggested that parts of the town tended to trade with certain areas, or displayed cultural preferences in the types of pottery used.

One essential commodity which must have been traded widely within Viking Age England is salt. By this period an elaborate network of packhorse and cart routes had developed associated with the Droitwich salt industry. Upwich was first documented in 962, and Middlewich soon afterwards. During the tenth century there was a proliferation of industrial activity as each site developed its own brine wells (Hurst 1997).

SHIPS AND SHIPPING

Despite the importance of land routes plied by packhorses and carts, most trade in bulk commodities would have depended upon river and sea transport. Our image of Viking Age shipping is dominated by the dragon-headed longship. In fact there was a wide variety of craft, each with different functions. A table of harbour dues for Billingsgate *c.*1000 distinguishes between three classes of vessel: a small ship, which was charged ½d; a larger ship with sails, charged 1d; and a barque or merchantman, charged 4d.

The first group probably included simple log-boats, like that excavated at Clapton (Greater London). Such boats were fairly workmanlike affairs, normally hollowed out of half of a split oak trunk, following a north-European tradition going back to prehistoric dugouts. Indeed, it has often been assumed that they were pre-Roman, until scientific dating methods proved otherwise. Tree-ring dating of the Clapton boat showed it was carved from a tree chopped down in the tenth century. The Clapton log-boat was 3.75m long by 0.65m wide; a replica could carry up to four people. It was propelled by paddle, with a bulkhead in the centre acting as a seat for the rower (Marsden *et al.* 1989). Four such boats have now been recovered in the London area from the river Lea, plus a curved oak rib from the Thames Exchange site which could have come from a small planked boat, or a light dugout with extended sides. Nine eleventh-century logboats have been recovered from the rivers Mersey and Irwell, indicating the degree of river traffic during the Viking Age. Most may have been used primarily for ferrying, fishing, fowling, and reed-gathering, but the range in length, 2.75-4.65m, suggests that some, such as examples from Irlam and Warrington, may have functioned as bulk-cargo carriers over short distances (McGrail 1978; McGrail and Switsur 1979).

The second group, of small vessels with sails, would have been more suitable for longer river journeys or short sea crossings. The Graveney boat is an example of an excavated boat belonging to this category (Fenwick 1978). She was a clinker-built merchant vessel, constructed *c.*927, 14m long and with a beam of 3.9m, which could have carried some 6-7 tons of cargo. Residues of hops may represent a cargo from Kent being carried up the Thames Estuary, whilst her ballast of unfinished lava millstones may reflect North Sea crossings. At some point in her career the keel had been repaired after having been badly cracked, perhaps from beaching with a heavy cargo on board. The Graveney boat was finally abandoned *c*.950 more than 1km from the sea in a creek alongside an improvised jetty of upright posts. Fragments of up to four similar ships have been found on the London waterfront; one find, from the Vintry site, suggested the vessel had been rigged for sailing.

The third category, of ocean-going vessels, probably included foreign vessels from northern Europe and Scandinavia. No complete vessels of this period have been recovered from English waters, although finds from the Thames Exchange site, including a carved mast partner which would have supported a mast up to 0.45m in diameter, show that such large vessels visited Viking Age London. It has also become clear that substantial clinker-built boats were being built in the Scandinavian tradition in the British Isles during the Viking Age. Tree-ring analysis has shown that one of the longships scuttled in the Roskilde fjord, Denmark, was made from timber grown in Ireland, and a substantial fragment of a large boat incorporated into the construction of the harbour at Tiel, in the Netherlands, had been built from timbers felled in south-east England 979-1008. The ship had evidently been burnt out and it is tempting to see it as a casualty of the documented Viking raid on Tiel in 1006-7 (Sarfatij 1999, 273).

COINAGE

The emergence of commercial trade is often seen as requiring a monetary economy, but we should recognise that in the early medieval period there were other methods of exchange. The role of coins and the nature of its production was very different from today. During the last quarter of the eighth century a regular English coinage based on the silver penny was established by Offa of Mercia. This developed into a proper currency which had a face value far in excess of its silver value. In eighth- and ninth-century Northumbria there was also a copper coinage comprising low denomination stycas but this was terminated by the arrival of the Vikings in the late ninth century.

The coinage of Anglo-Saxon England was not supplied by a central mint issuing to the whole kingdom (Dolley 1976). Coin production was decentralised, carried out in a number of mints, each based in a *burh*. At each mint a number of private individuals, men of substance in the community, acted as moneyers, taking responsibility for the coinage, on behalf of royal authority. The number of these moneyers varies according to the importance of the mint, but only in very important towns were there more than ten operating at once. It was established practice that pennies should carry on their obverse the name of the ruler whose authority was recognised at their place of minting, and on the reverse the name of the moneyer.

The role of moneyers and the nature of Viking Age coin production has been greatly illuminated by the Coppergate finds (*plate 16*). An iron coin die of the St Peter's issue, *c.*921-7, bearing a sword and hammer and a dedication to St Peter, was found discarded amongst the rubbish in the metal-working workshops (Pirie 1986). The die was cylindrical in shape, flaring outwards at the base, where a tang protruded which could be fixed into a bench or anvil. The head had been specially hardened. Nearby there were also two lead trial pieces, or test strikings, and the cap of a die for a penny of Æthelstan (927-39). It is possible that the Coppergate excavations accidentally stumbled upon the site of a mint, although the insubstantial nature of the timber workshops is not what anyone had imagined a tenth-century mint would look like. It seems more plausible that only the die production and engraving were carried out here. Nevertheless, the workshops must have operated under the authority of moneyers, as the dies could not be allowed to fall into the wrong hands. The remains were found in two adjacent tenements, occupied by craftsmen with wide experience in metalworking. The finds must cover a 20-30 year time span, indicating some continuity of production. The lead trial pieces may have been tests, the damaged dies may have been returned for recasting. However, the discovery of a further lead trial piece for a penny of Eadwig (955-9), by the Chester moneyer Frothric, prompts an alternative explanation for the trial pieces and it has been suggested that this may have been a customs seal to show that import duty had been paid at the port of entry.

From the death of Offa in 796 to Burgred's defeat by the Vikings in 874, the bulk of coinage was produced at, and circulated from, three cities: London, Canterbury and Rochester. During this period there was a rapid expansion in the number of moneyers, reflecting the growing need for coinage because of increased economic activity. The Danelaw was originally poorly served by mints, but by the early tenth century mints were operating in Bedford, Chester, Derby, Leicester and Nottingham, as well as York and Lincoln.

As Viking leaders took political control they started to mint their own coins for propaganda purposes. Although coins were not being issued in the Scandinavian homelands at this point, after his baptism Guthrum adopted Anglo-Saxon traditions and issued coins in the name of Athelstan, based on the coinage of Alfred. By the 890s silver pennies were being circulated in the eastern Danelaw bearing the legend 'St Edmund', in memory of the East Anglian king martyred by the Danes in 870. According to the monk Abbo of Fleury, Edmund had been tied to a tree, lashed with whips, and pierced with arrows. The reasons for this apparent U-turn, in which Vikings newly converted to Christianity recognised their victim as a saint, must have been largely political. What better way to overtake the cult of the martyr as a focus for potential opposition than to adopt the saint of the East Angles as their own? Cnut and Sithric had coins struck in York from *c.*890 following Carolingian designs; some bore the legend 'St Peter'; others carried religious motifs (Dolley 1978). By the second quarter of the tenth century York was issuing more recognisably 'Viking' coins with Norse legends and pagan motifs such as the raven, swords, and Thor's hammer (*plate 15*). After the expulsion of Erik Bloodaxe in 954, however, York was absorbed into mainstream English minting practice. From *c.*920, Lincoln also started minting coins, in the name of St Martin.

Nevertheless, single finds of coins (as opposed to hoards) indicate a general decline in the usage of coins over the ninth century (Blackburn 1993). This need not indicate a general economic recession, for people may have found alternative means of conducting transactions. It is also possible that some items circulated within a full monetary system, whilst others were available for barter or credit. A lot would depend on whether transactions could rely on personal trust or were purely commercial. The population did not, apparently, have full confidence in the new coins, which in many areas were only accepted for their silver content and not their face value, as demonstrated by surface pecking to test their silver content. Many transactions may have been conducted by weight of silver.

There are 32 *burhs* in which post-1960 excavations have produced Viking Age deposits but no coins; there are 23 *burhs* where coins have been found, but only four with more than ten: York, Lincoln, Northampton and Winchester. There was a mint in Bedford from the mid-tenth century at least, but no coin finds until the twelfth century, despite substantial excavation. In Northampton, the tenth- and eleventh-century levels at Chalk Lane yielded *c.*9000 potsherds, *c.*5000 animal bones, and 4 coins; at St Peter's Street there were *c.*1500 potsherds, *c.*2500 animal bones, and 6 coins (Hinton 1986). Of course, both pottery and animals (apart from a few hens and pigs) also had to be acquired by trade. Both commodities can be as much a record of transactions as coins, but could have been exchanged by barter with no coins changing hands. Rural sites also yield few coins in the tenth century. Viking Age levels at Portchester yielded *c.*11,000 animal bones and 2 coins; those at Cheddar *c.*1000 bones and 5 coins. Folding scales identical to those from Chester and York (*plate 17*) have been found at Goltho and North Elmham.

Finds of silver ingots, such as those discovered by metal detector from near Easingwold (North Yorkshire), suggest that even within the immediate hinterland of York a bullion economy may have been operating in the late ninth and early tenth centuries. At Cottam (East Yorkshire) only a handful of coins have been recovered from the tenth-century settlement, compared to the scores of copper-alloy stycas from the eighth- and ninth-century enclosure. However, a number of circular lead weights have been recovered from the later site, which probably indicate the weighing of silver.

The payment of rent was the other major mechanism whereby wealth changed hands. In Middle Saxon England rent was normally paid in kind. One of the earliest records of rent being paid to a royal estate is to Offa of Mercia by the church at Worcester, dated 793-6: 'two tuns full of pure ale and a coomb full of mild ale and a coomb full of Welsh ale, and seven oxen six wethers and 40 cheeses and sixe long theru [untrans] and 30 ambers of unground corn and four ambers of meal'. Whilst rent was paid in perishable goods it was fairly inconvenient, as the king had to travel around his estate in order to eat up his rents. Paying in coin was simpler, and by the time of the Domesday Book most rents had been at least partly commuted to money.

In 973 Edgar reformed the coinage, giving coins a six-year period of use, after which they were no longer legal tender. The king took a profit each time the currency was reminted; therefore Edgar's reforms served to maximise royal profits. He also prohibited the circulation of foreign coins; all silver entering the kingdom was to be reminted and had to bear the king's head. By the late tenth century the production of coin took place at 50-60 mints operating up and down the country. Æthelstan further regulated the minting of coins by stipulating that 'there shall be one coinage throughout the king's realm, and no man shall mint money except in a town'.

By the eleventh century coinage was in general use, but it is difficult to quantify its importance for the general populace. It has been suggested that finds of pennies cut into halves and quarters in deposits in London and York shows that coins were being used for small change in everyday transactions. However, whilst a penny might sound like small change to us we have to remember that during the Viking Age it was worth a reasonable amount.

During the eleventh century the continuous heavy wastage from the currency through the export of coin was counterbalanced by the inflow of silver in payment for exports. Despite the continued threat of Viking raids, mints continued to operate at a large number of locations, although sometimes, as at the hillfort at Cadbury, they were taken inside strongly fortified sites.

In conclusion, the Vikings appear to have had a mixed effect on trade. International trade was disrupted, although some Scandinavians made their living by acting as middlemen for the importation of exotic goods. Internal trade grew in response to new urban markets, and although there was a decline in small-scale monetary transactions in the ninth century these appear to have been replaced by non-monetary forms of exchange. Aspects of the Viking Age economy would have been far more socially embedded than a modern market economy and many transactions may have had a social dimension. Later literary sources testify to the importance of gift exchange and the giving of silver rings as a means of rewarding followers and winning their continued allegiance. In Viking Age England land as well as goods may have changed hands in return for services.

9

CHURCHES AND MONASTERIES

When the Vikings arrived in the British Isles they found a land which had long been Christian. In England a network of minster churches is believed to have grown up during the seventh and eighth centuries and now covered the country. These included major town buildings such as Edwin's Minster in York, or the church discovered by excavation in Cirencester, and smaller churches attached to rural aristocratic sites. In Atlantic Britain – the south-west peninsula, Wales, the Lake District, and south-west Scotland – Christian roots were deeper still, reaching back at least to the fifth or sixth centuries, and probably to the Christianity of Late Roman Britain. On the Isle of Man it is believed that the system of keeils, or small Christian chapels, was already in place. Similar small chapels were also being built in the south-west from the eighth century onwards.

In all areas monasteries provided a focus for Christian worship, but to the Vikings they were little more than unprotected storehouses of treasure. Although there are instances of

Christian Anglo-Saxon leaders attacking religious sites, notably King Eadred who destroyed Ripon in 948, the Church had generally been able to depend upon spiritual sanctions for its safety. Viking raiders had no respect for such conventions, although there is little evidence that the plundering of churches by Vikings stemmed from any pagan hatred of Christianity. It was simply that they were regarded as relatively easy sources of portable wealth, and also perhaps that for the initial raiding parties they provided a good means of probing the strength of English defences.

MONASTERIES

Monastic sites were particularly vulnerable to attack. Anglo-Saxon monasteries were frequently major land-owners and by the eighth century had also amassed considerable portable wealth of their own, as well as often being entrusted with treasure by Anglo-Saxon kings. The eremitic origins of monastic life meant that some early monasteries were sited on isolated coastal sites, with no hope of defence against attack from the sea.

In Northumbria the exposed coastal sites at Tynemouth, Hartlepool, Whitby, Monkwearmouth, Jarrow and Lindisfarne all appear to have been largely abandoned in the ninth century. Historical sources recount how the community of St Cuthbert, displaced from Lindisfarne, wandered for several years before finding a new home at Chester-le-Street. Hexham and Whithorn ceased to function as bishoprics and even York was reduced to relative poverty. Excavations at Beverley have demonstrated that the monastery was abandoned in the mid-ninth century; a hoard of *c.*851 comprising 23 Northumbrian stycas buried in a leather purse coincides with the first year the Viking army overwintered (Armstrong *et al.* 1991). Further south the bishoprics of Dunwich, Elmham and Lindsey came to an effective end; the bishop's throne at North Elmham dramatically blackened by smoke. Exposed Kentish monasteries also disappear from the record, including Reculver, Dover and Folkestone. In the London area, Woking and Bermondsey did not survive into the tenth century, and Barking Abbey was burnt down.

However, it is difficult to establish both how far such decline was the direct result of Viking attack, and also how far religious life may still have continued at some of these sites. Some communities certainly collapsed because Vikings seized their estates; others disappeared because of the replacement of the local aristocracy by Vikings who did not share their religious convictions. Along the border between Wessex and the Danelaw, Ælfred seized monastic lands to act as a buffer zone against the Vikings. In short, the Viking Age brought about a level of redistribution of monastic land comparable to the Dissolution in the sixteenth century. Nevertheless, it would be a mistake to attribute the ninth-century monastic decline entirely to the Vikings; there was general concern for falling standards and even Ælfred did not blame the Vikings for the poor state of learning in England's monastic houses. Rather, he saw them as a punishment for earlier backsliding. Hartlepool ceased to function before the Viking raids, and although Jarrow and Monkwearmouth were apparently destroyed by fire, this could have been at the hands of the Scots, and there appears to have been some continuing religious presence into the Late Anglo-Saxon period.

After the disruption of the Viking raids and settlements there was growing enthusiasm in the tenth century for a reform of monasticism based on the Benedictine rule. This was encouraged first by Edmund and then Edgar, both believing that the spiritual support of the Church would be valuable to them. Old communities, including Beverley, Glastonbury, Ripon, Winchester and Worcester, were reformed and new ones founded. In the second half of the tenth century the foundation and endowment of monasteries underwent rapid growth throughout eastern and southern England.

MINSTER CHURCHES

Minster churches frequently originated as monastic communities; the Old English *mynster* is derived from the Latin *monasterium*. By the Viking Age their function may have evolved into that of a church serving a congregation, with a community of clergy responsible for the pastoral care of a large area (Blair 1988; Radford 1973). Priests may have been sent out to preach to local communities and the laity would come for baptism and burial. Minster churches may also have been founded by the aristocracy in the middle of their estates. Early royal minsters were often set within their own precinct enclosures, a little way from the royal palace. At Cheddar, for example, the ninth-century minster and palace were placed *c.*200m apart, while at Bampton (Oxfordshire) traces of a large enclosure have been recognised. This was not always the case; St Peter's, Gloucester, was sited within the town with the royal palace at Kingsholm outside the walls.

In fact, as we have already seen (chapter 4) many of the new Anglo-Saxon towns grew around minster churches. The developing road system funnelled traffic to them, and markets were established at their gates. At Bampton excavation has revealed an urban style of cellared building, south of the church enclosure, adjacent to a possible early market area (Blair 1998).

The wealth of minster churches depended on their monopoly as recipients of fees for burial, and a variety of other dues. Many retained, or claimed, exclusive burial rights until well after the Norman Conquest. St Oswald's, Gloucester, for example, continued in importance, probably competing with only three or four other parish churches. At Winchester, the main cemetery was confined within the walls of the Old Minster until the fourteenth century. Nevertheless, the minsters were threatened by the rise of parish churches in the tenth century and gradually lost their special position.

PARISH CHURCHES

The creation of rural parishes and parish churches went hand in hand with the fragmentation of the great estates during the Viking Age (see chapter 3). The foundation of new local churches had been taking place spasmodically from the eighth century, but the great age of church building took place in the tenth and eleventh centuries. In fact, the construction of most new churches is thought by some to have taken place within the space of a few decades of 1000. By the time of the Domesday Book there were demonstrably over 2600 local churches, and arguably several thousands more. Probably almost 500 of these survive to the present day in some form or other (Morris 1989).

This boom in the construction of churches was a by-product of the new landowners' quest for status. The possession of a church was an important status symbol, as well as a source of income. Noblemen also attempted to acquire burial rights for their churches, reserved until then by the old minster churches, so that their families could be buried on their estates, in the same way that pagan cemeteries had developed around ancestral graves. The new churches were therefore normally attached to the manorial residence, as at Raunds, where the church was built adjacent to the manorial enclosure. A survey within the Archdeaconry of Colchester has revealed that out of a total of 29 churches of definite Saxon origin, 19 are alongside later manorial halls.

Church foundations therefore frequently pre-date the development of the village, although as the manorial churches acquired burial and baptismal rights they also acquired the functions of a parish church. In many areas the modern parish boundaries may preserve the pre-Conquest manorial boundaries. The ecclesiastical dues derived from the performance of burial and baptism would frequently have supported a parish priest, which in turn brought about significant changes in the organisation of Christianity as the priests were now brought into daily face-to-face contact with their parishioners.

Most of the manorial churches were new buildings, although some were adapted from existing minster or monastic sites. Many probably began as wooden buildings, but from the eleventh century most were soon transformed into impressive stone edifices. Richard Gem (1988) has argued for a 'great rebuilding' in stone of churches beginning during the reign of Edward the Confessor, but continuing until the twelfth century. The new churches generally started as simple small rectangular boxes providing a nave only, although chancels were often added later. At Wharram Percy there is some evidence to suggest that an eighth- or ninth-century minster or monastery may have fallen into disuse as a result of Viking disruption. A small timber church was established on a new site in the tenth century (*plate 33*), perhaps as a private chapel of an Anglo-Scandinavian lord. This was enlarged in the eleventh century by a small two-celled church consisting of a nave and chancel. The church became a focus for burials of the early lords of the Percy manor, and later of the parish (Bell *et al.* 1987).

At Raunds Furnells (Northamptonshire) a small single-celled late ninth- or tenth-century church was erected on a stone foundation adjacent to the manorial enclosure (Boddington 1996). Initially this tiny chapel was without a graveyard and provides an example of the seigneurial provision of a church as one of the key attributes of those seeking the status of a *thegn*. The church acquired burial rights during the tenth century and an enclosure ditch was cut defining a rect-angular graveyard, 30m x 40m. The addition of a graveyard may also reflect the rising status of the owner, and an early grave under a decorated stone slab, perhaps with a stone cross at its head, is a good contender for the founder's grave. At this stage a chancel was also added to the church and excavation has revealed a clergy bench within the chancel, a canopied altar at the east end of the nave and, in front of the altar, a *sacrarium*, a pottery vessel placed in the floor to serve as a piscina or soakaway for holy water. A wooden bellcote stood against the west wall. By now the church must have served a broader community than those who occupied the manor house itself, and it has been suggested that the cemetery was drawn from a population of about 40, including a range of social status (chapter 10). In the late eleventh or early twelfth century this building was replaced by a larger church, 15m long, presumably to accommodate a larger congregation using this as their parish church. The Domesday Book records the transfer of the manor from Burgred to the Bishop of Coutances at the Norman Conquest. The rebuilding of the church, levelling of the graveyard (chapter 10) and rough treatment of Saxon crosses may correspond to this transfer of ownership.

Many of the new churches were founded by Scandinavian lords. The sequestration of monastic estates in the Danelaw may even have facilitated the creation of local churches as some minsters lost control of their territories. At several Yorkshire sites the lords chose to record their benefactions in a prominent position on the church sundial, for all to read (Wall 1997; Watts *et al.* 1997). At Aldborough (North Yorkshire) the Old English inscription records that 'Ulf ordered the church to be put up for himself and for Gunwaru's soul.' At St Gregory's Minster, Kirkdale (North Yorkshire), it commemorates that another lord with a Norse name, Orm, bought the redundant minster and erected a new church on its site during 1055-65. Excavations have revealed a number of graves in the field to the north of the present churchyard, under ridge and furrow plough soil containing eleventh and twelfth-century pottery. Burials excavated on either side of the tower were on a different alignment from

13 Sundial, St Gregory's Minster, Kirkdale. The inscription records that 'Orm, son of Gamal, acquired the church of St Gregory when it was tumbled and ruined, and had it rebuilt from the ground in honour of Christ and St Gregory, in the days of Edward the King and Tosti the Earl'. The sundial shows the day divided into eight tides of three hours each. Lines mark the middle of the tides; it also has an extra line marking the start of the morning tide at 7.30 a.m., no doubt the time at which Mass was held

that of the present church, but were on a similar alignment to those excavated in the field, suggesting a major reorganisation of the site and contraction of the churchyard, possibly associated with the eleventh-century takeover and rebuilding (Rahtz and Watts 1998).

URBAN CHURCHES

There was a similar boom in church building in the towns. These new churches were linked to the wealth of towns and the presence of an urban aristocracy. Many were simple single-cell structures, functioning as private household chapels for urban 'estates'; others may have been founded by groups of citizens. They were sometimes slow to acquire burial and other parochial rights, which were preserved by the urban minsters. Churches proliferated in towns such as

Lincoln, London, York, Norwich and Winchester, although
their number may be linked to the number of estates and
the wealth of local lords rather than the size of population.
In London there were 30 churches by the Norman
Conquest; in Norwich there were 24. Most were sited on
former domestic tenements in prominent positions on street
frontages and particularly at the junctions of major streets.
Recorded property disputes reveal that urban churches
were treated as private property which could be inherited
or bought and sold. Simple rectangular stone structures
representing eleventh-century urban churches have been
excavated at the site of St Mark's, Lincoln (Gilmour and
Stocker 1986); St Nicholas Shambles, London (White 1988);
and, perhaps of the tenth century, St Helen-on-the-Walls,
York (Magilton 1980). Excavations at Lower Brook Street
in Winchester uncovered two small churches close together;
St Mary's occupied a small plot alongside the street, while
St Pancras was away from the main street, behind the yards
and approached by a path. Urban churches had their own
favoured locations, such as adjacent to a market or beside a
town gate.

Many urban churches may also have been founded by
Scandinavian settlers. There are churches dedicated to the
Norwegian saint, Olaf, in Chester, York, Exeter, Norwich,
Southwark, Chichester, Grimsby and London. The Anglo-
Saxon Chronicle records for 1055 that 'In this year passed
away earl Siward at York, and he was buried in Galmanho in
the church which he himself had built and consecrated in the
name of God and [St] Olaf'. At St Mary Castlegate, York, a late
tenth- or early eleventh-century dedication stone reveals that
two of the church's patrons had Norse names. In Denmark,

dedications to St Clement, the patron saint of sailors, became popular after the conversion. In England there is a preponderance of St Clement dedications in the east and south-east, particularly in urban areas. Barbara Crawford has argued that these frequently represent eleventh-century garrison churches, established by Knutr's Scandinavian military elite. Many are at strategic locations, near river crossing points or town gates. St Clement Danes, London, is located outside the west entrance to the city on the route to Westminster, and probably close to the Danish royal residence.

In both town and country, therefore, the Viking Age witnessed church foundation on a massive scale and the crystallisation of the parish system. Changes in ecclesiastical structure mirror those in land ownership. The monopoly of the monasteries and minsters was broken as the old estates were fragmented. New secular landowners sought to demonstrate their power and wealth by the construction of private churches. Later they would tend to endow a chapel within an existing church, but for the present each manor had its own chapel, which would be used for burial. Such displays were not confined to Saxon lords, and Viking settlers competed to demonstrate their authority. Indeed, the changes in land ownership which led to this spate of church building may have been a direct consequence of the Scandinavian settlement.

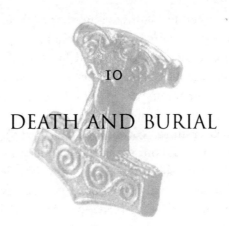

10

DEATH AND BURIAL

It is one of the most remarkable aspects of Viking Age England that despite several centuries of Scandinavian settlement there are very few Viking graves. As testament of an earlier invasion of pagan Anglo-Saxon immigrants, there are vast communal cemeteries, each one containing hundreds and even thousands of cremations, and inhumation cemeteries of warriors and their women laid out with their weaponry and dressed in their folk costume. Yet for the ninth and tenth centuries there are less than 25 known burial sites in England which have been described as Scandinavian, and the majority of these comprise single burials, frequently accompanied by only one or two artefacts.

In Scandinavia, on the other hand, there was a revival of elaborate burial rites in the Viking Age, as Paganism came into conflict with Christianity. In the areas from which the Vikings came there was no standard burial custom and there seems to have been a wide variety of local practices. The dead were either inhumed or cremated with their possessions, and sometimes placed in coffins, or in a burial chamber, or on a bier of some sort. There were great ship burials, such as those discovered at Oseberg and Gokstad in Norway, but there is no evidence that ships were ever set alight and floated out to sea. Warriors were often buried with their horse and weapons (although not their armour, as once dead they could be killed any number of times without further harm!). Well-to-do females would be laid out with their jewellery, and sometimes a wagon to take them to the next world. Sacrificial offerings of food and drink, and even human slaves, have also been found. Provision was being made for a further life of feasting and fighting in Valhalla.

The presence of grave-goods has often been interpreted as indicating a pagan custom and such accompanied burials have frequently been described as Viking. However, if the various candidates for Scandinavian burial in England are mapped (*14*) then it is apparent that there are at least two distinct trends. In north-west England and Cumbria there is a cluster of burials, sometimes under mounds and frequently with an assortment of weapons. These burials should really be seen as part of a distribution of Norse burials in the areas bordering on the Irish Sea; they reflect a similar culture to that known from the Isle of Man where there is a relatively large number of highly visible Norse burials. A number of possible outliers to this group can be found spreading across the Pennines to the Viking Kingdom of York, where they become intermingled with less characteristically Norse burials.

By contrast, in those areas of lowland England which became known as the Danelaw there are very few strong candidates for Scandinavian burials. With the exception of

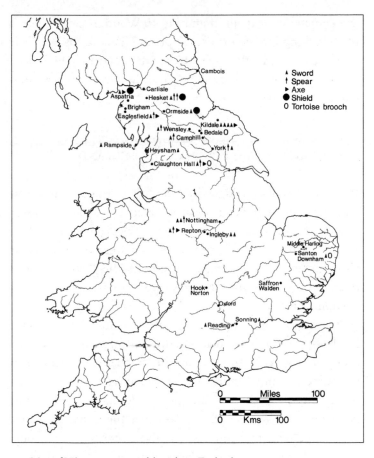

Sword ▲
Spear †
Axe ►
Shield ●
Tortoise brooch 0

Cambois

Aspatria ▲ ● • Carlisle
• Hesket ▲ † † ●
• Brigham • Ormside ▲ ● ●
Eaglesfield ▲ ►
▲ † Wensley • Kildale ▲ ▲ ▲ ▲ ►
▲ † Bedale 0
▲ † Camphill
▲ Rampside •
• Heysham ▲ † York † ▲
• Claughton Hall ▲ † ► 0

▲ ▲ † Nottingham •
▲ † ► Repton • Ingleby ▲ ▲

Middle Harling •
• Santon
Downham ▲ 0

Hook •
Norton
Saffron •
Walden

• Oxford
▲ Reading • Sonning ▲

0 ——— Miles ——— 100
0 ——— Kms ——— 100

14 Map of Viking accompanied burials in England

the cemeteries at Repton and Heath Wood, Ingleby, the rest of the Viking burial corpus comprises a handful of burials in churchyards and other Late Saxon cemeteries which have been singled out as unusual because they have been accompanied by artefacts.

SCANDINAVIAN-STYLE BURIALS IN ENGLAND

Ben Edwards has catalogued Viking burials in the north-west, and the following description is based upon his discussion (1998), and on earlier accounts by Cowen (1948; 1967) and Shetelig (1940). Many of these burials were investigated in the eighteenth and nineteenth centuries; the finds have often been lost, and we must often rely upon unreliable antiquarian accounts of their discovery.

A mound at Beacon Hill, Aspatria (Cumbria), some 9m in diameter, was examined in the late eighteenth century and found to contain a stone cist or chamber, comprising six stones, within which was a skeleton. The finds were published in 1792 and although they have subsequently been lost we can be fairly certain that the grave contained a skeleton with a sword with a silver encrusted hilt and a spearhead with a decorated silver socket. In addition, an ordinary axe is illustrated and 'pieces of a shield' are referred to in the description of the find. More unusual is the presence of a gold buckle and a strap-end of Carolingian type, confirming the high status of the deceased, further underlined by an iron horse-bit and spur.

At Hesket-in-the-Forest (Cumbria) a layer of charcoal, bones and ashes with several grave-goods was found in 1822 lying on a bed of sand under a cairn, 7m in diameter (*plate 18*). All the burnt bones were of animals which had been cremated as part of the burial rite; there was no trace of a human skeleton. The weapons had been deliberately damaged. The sword and spears were bent; the shield had been broken in two; the sword had been deliberately bent back twice on itself by heating and hammering, rendering it useless. Horse and weapons may also have been thrown on the cremation pyre as it was reported that the sword, shield boss and horse-bit were all burnt. There was also an axe head, a pair of spurs, a fine unburnt comb with its protective comb case, a sickle and a whetstone.

A third mound burial was also discovered in 1822 at Claughton Hall, Garstang (Lancashire), when a small sand mound was cut through in the course of road building. The objects comprised a pair of gilt copper alloy oval brooches, apparently wrapped up back-to-back in cloth and encasing two beads and a molar tooth, a Carolingian silver mount re-used as a brooch, and various iron objects, including a sword, spear, axe and hammer (*plate 35*). This may have been a double burial of male and female, but it is more likely that the burial was male and the brooches enclosed a ritual deposit of various amulets or keepsakes. There may have been a wooden chamber below the surface but the finds also included a Bronze Age axe hammer and a pot containing a cremation, now lost, so the finds from Claughton may represent another Scandinavian cremation, or secondary usage of a prehistoric barrow.

A small number of other sites in the north-west have also been advanced as Scandinavian burials, but only that at Eaglesfield (Cumbria) is likely to have been a mound burial.

A skeleton accompanied by a sword, a spearhead (described as a 'halberd'), and possibly a ring-headed cloak pin (described as a 'fibula') was found on the limestone crags in 1814.

Outside Cumbria, Scandinavian barrow burials are extremely rare in England. At Cambois, Bedlington (Northumberland), three bodies were found in a cist-grave in a mound (Alexander 1987). One was a female, aged 45–60; the other two were males, the first in his twenties, and the second in his forties. The only grave-goods were an enamelled disc brooch and a bone comb. Lack of weapons perhaps suggests that these may have been relatively peaceful landowners; they are certainly a Viking Age elite in an area with little other evidence for their presence. Further south, a sword and spear buried with a skeleton in a natural hill at Camphill, near Bedale (North Yorkshire), may represent the choice of a natural prominence for a burial to avoid erecting a mound. There is an antiquarian report that in 1723 a skeleton, horse bit and an iron knife with a bone handle were found in the middle of the top of Silbury Hill (Wiltshire), but the finds are now lost and this is impossible to date to the Viking Age. Another possible Viking mound burial has been identified at Hook Norton (Oxfordshire), where skeletons were found associated with a late ninth-century coin hoard (Biddle and Blair 1987).

Such individual burials represent a distinct tradition of Scandinavian pagan burial which is parallelled especially in Norway, and examples of which are also found in the Northern and Western Isles of Scotland, as well as the Isle of Man. This north-west group reflects uncontrolled isolated burial away from churchyards and outside the control of authority. Such burials often seek to become part of the landscape, frequently by the use of mounds, which are generally interpreted as reflecting claims to land, and the evocation of ancient traditions. There are other candidates for single burials which must also represent pagan Scandinavian practice, and which may once have been marked by mounds or some other distinctive feature, although no structural evidence survives. Stirrups, shears, horseshoe and prick-spur were found in 1884 near Magdalen Bridge in Oxford. Originally thought to have been casual losses they have recently been reinterpreted as the remains of a Viking warrior and his horse, buried on an island in the Cherwell around 1000, although this interpretation must still be regarded as disputed. The horseshoe and a third small stirrup are seen as later intrusive objects but two larger stirrups with brass overlay, the prick-spur and shears are each seen as consistent with a pattern of late tenth-century equestrian burials in Jutland. If so then this is one of the last furnished warrior burials known from England. The man may have belonged to one of the armies that raided the region in the 990s, or even to Svein Forkbeard's army which attacked Oxford in 1009 and 1013. It may be significant that the burial site is close to St Clement's, the possible site of a Knutr-period Danish 'garrison' (Blair and Crawford 1997).

HEATH WOOD, INGLEBY AND REPTON: TWO VIKING CEMETERIES IN THE EAST MIDLANDS

The only other mound burials from England come from the unique site at Heath Wood, Ingleby (Derbyshire), where there is the only known Scandinavian cremation cemetery in the British Isles. Here there are some 59 barrows on a commanding site on a natural ridge overlooking the river Trent, 1.2km (¾ mile) from the river (15). Although the site has become known as Ingleby it is in fact some distance from the modern village, whose name may indeed reflect an 'English village', noted as unusual in an area which was under Scandinavian control. In total 20 or approximately one third of the mounds have been excavated. Thomas Bateman, the notable Peak District barrow digger, records that he opened five on 22 May 1855, presumably at the invitation of his hosts at nearby Foremark Hall. Bateman found that each covered the site of a funeral pyre, upon which burnt human bones remained as they had been left by fire. Further work in the 1940s and 50s confirmed the presence of cremation hearths, but also indicated that some of the mounds were apparently empty. The mounds were generally 9m in diameter and several contained cremation hearths, often in stone settings, about 1.8m in diameter (*plate 34*). The hearths comprised a layer of charcoal and burnt bone. This included the remains of both men and women, as well as sacrificial animal offerings including cattle, sheep, dog, and possibly horse and pig. A number of grave-goods were found mixed in with the burnt remains, including two mutilated swords, iron buckles, and a copper alloy strap-end. In one mound there were the remains of an iron spade, three nails and wire embroidery, comparable to finds from ninth- and tenth-century graves at Birka in Sweden (Posnansky 1956; Richards *et al.* 1995).

Excavation of Mounds 50 and 56 in 1998-2000 has further demonstrated the presence both of human cremation and animal sacrifice, but has thrown doubt on the existence of

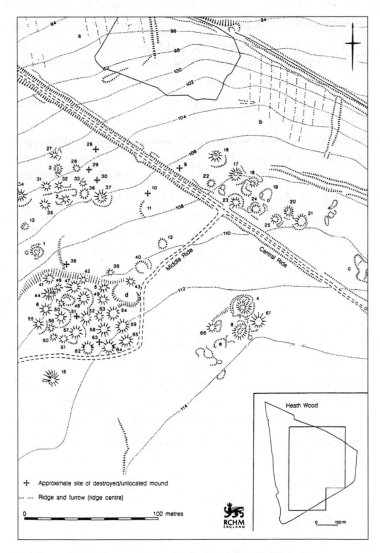

15 Plan of Viking barrow cemetery, Heath Wood, Ingleby (Derbyshire).
Courtesy English Heritage

empty cenotaph mounds. Mound 50 contained the cremated remains of an adult human and several animals, as well as the unburnt jaw of a cow, and a horse tooth. A cow skull was also found in the neighbouring Mound 6. A variety of nails and tacks and badly burnt copper alloy objects were recovered from the cremation hearth, including a hinge plate from a coffin or chest. The mound had been constructed by levelling an area down to bedrock, and then dumping a circular platform of clean sand, *c*.0.1m in depth. Upon this the funeral pyre had been constructed. Following this, sand and stone quarried from the surrounding area had been heaped to create a substantial mound, upon which a soil or turf line developed. The neighbouring Mound 56 had also been built from the natural bedrock but contained no levelling layer of clean sand. Initially no trace of a burial was found but in the final season of excavation a small patch of cremated human bone was found associated with a well-preserved Hiberno-Norse ring-headed pin on the edge of the barrow. This does not appear to have been derived from a central cremation pyre but was instead placed deliberately on the ground surface before Mound 56 was constructed. This discovery suggests that all of the mounds may originally have contained burials, but that these small peripheral cremations could easily have been missed in earlier investigations, giving rise to the cenotaph theory. The presence of the ring-headed pin is also of interest. It is the first from a burial in England outside Cumbria, and could indicate a Hiberno-Norse connection. Examination of the relationship of a number of mounds in the main cluster has demonstrated that these mounds were constructed on the same surface and suggests that they are broadly contemporary. It is proposed that the cemetery was in use for a relatively brief period of time, and probably for no more than 20-30 years. Indeed, the most likely scenario is that the cemetery was created in a single act. Although cremation is rare in England there are cremation barrow cemeteries from northern Jutland and from Sweden and the site should be understood in the context of the over-wintering of the Viking Great Army at Repton.

Heath Wood is only 4km (2.5 miles) to the south-west of Repton, where the over-wintering of the Viking army saw the construction of a fortified camp and the transformation of a royal mausoleum into a charnel house (chapter 2). As well as the mass burial, a number of Scandinavian style burials have been excavated at the east end of the church at Repton. Although adjacent to the church these burials were beyond the contemporary limits of the monastic cemetery. The earliest grave was of a man aged at least 35-40, who had been killed by a massive cut to the top of his left leg. He wore a necklace of two glass beads and a silver Thor's hammer amulet. By his side was a sword in a leather bound wooden scabbard with a fleece lining, a folding knife, and a key. A wild boar's tusk and a jackdaw bone had been carefully placed between his thighs; the former may be seen as symbolically replacing what had been cut off by the sword blow. If the boar's tusk is a sign of fertility, and the jackdaw bone a substitute for a raven then those burying the slain warrior next to the church were looking after his options with Frey and Odin, as well as with Thor, in addition to seeking the protection of the adjacent Christian shrine. A substantial post-hole at the eastern end of the grave suggests that it had been marked by a wooden post. Other graves were accompanied by knives and weapons; it is likely that an axe found

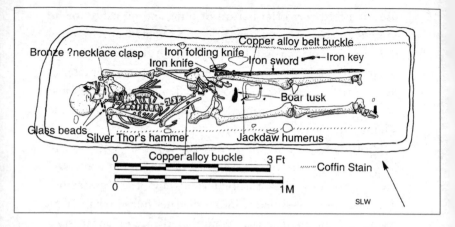

16 Grave 511, Repton (Derbyshire). This male burial was found north of the church, inside the line of Viking defences, but outside the monastic cemetery. The man had been killed by a massive cut to the head of the left femur (after Biddle and Kjølbye-Biddle 1992)

in the graveyard in 1922 also came from a grave. One burial was accompanied by five silver pennies and a gold finger ring, lying together beside the skull. The coins suggest a burial date in the 870s; it is likely that these were further burials of Viking warriors of the 'Great Army' which wintered at Repton in 873-4 (Biddle and Kjølbye-Biddle 1992).

Whilst the Heath Wood cemetery represents the maintenance of a pagan rite, incorporating animal sacrifice and cremation, in a hostile situation on an isolated hilltop, those buried at Repton deliberately sought to associate their dead with the Mercian royal and ecclesiastical complex. It is likely that both cemeteries are contemporary, but it might be that the two cemeteries represent a division in the Viking camp, one group preferring legitimation through association with the Mercian site; the other preferring traditional pagan values.

It might be significant that from Repton the army split into two bands. One group was tired of war and returned to Northumbria where in 876 Healfden and his men 'shared out the land of the Northumbrians, and they proceeded to plough and support themselves'. Guthrum, on the other hand, left Repton in 874 and marched on East Anglia and then Wessex.

CHURCHYARD AND CHRISTIAN CEMETERY BURIAL

Other Scandinavian burials have been identified on the basis of objects found in churchyards. Their interpretation is rather problematic. In the first place churchyards are inevitably heavily disturbed and the association between objects and a skeleton is rarely clear. Secondly, there is a tendency to categorise any accompanied grave as pagan and therefore Scandinavian, despite the lack of any documentary sources which would indicate that the Christian church prohibited the practice, and the fact that many of the objects are ostensibly Anglo-Saxon in style. Thirdly, the clear physical juxtaposition between Scandinavian and Christian burials does not in any case necessarily indicate a causal link. The burials may be adjacent, as in the case at Repton where the burials are adjacent to the church, but not in the area of the monastic cemetery, which only later spread over it. Or the burials may pre-date the use of the land by the Christian church, as may be the case at Kildale (Yorkshire) where seven or eight were observed when the floor of the church was removed in 1867. All were aligned east-west, and all were accompanied by grave-goods. One burial had a sword, tweezers, a silver-inlaid knife, and a set of scales; a burial found under the nave had an axe and there were at least three more with swords and knives (Elgee 1930).

The fact that a number of weapons have been recovered from churchyards in north-west England gives some support to the idea that whilst some pagan settlers in this area sought to legitimise claims to land through prominent mound burial, others chose to associate themselves with churchyard sites. It also indicates that there was a greater tendency to maintain the weapon burial practice in churchyards in an area where weapon burial was more widely practised anyway. A sword has been found in the churchyard at Rampside (Lancashire), and a sword, shield boss, iron bar and knife were found in the churchyard at Ormside in 1898. An elaborate silver bowl had been found at the same site at least 75 years later, and may represent a second grave, or earlier disturbance of an object from the same grave. There is also a record of an iron spearhead being found, about 1800, in the same place as a fine hogback stone in the churchyard of St Peter's at Heysham. When put alongside a female burial with a bone comb from the cemetery beside the adjacent chapel of St Patrick, it is suggestive of the presence of a number of accompanied burials (Potter and Andrews 1994). Similarly, a ring-headed cloak pin recovered from the churchyard at Brigham (Cumbria) may have originated in a burial. These burial rites were also maintained in the larger population centres and in the context of major ecclesiastical sites. A number of early tenth-century burials with grave-goods, including buckles, strap-ends and a small whetstone, were revealed by excavations at Carlisle Cathedral in 1988 (Keevill 1989).

Like mound burial, accompanied churchyard burials are also found across the Pennines in Yorkshire. As well as the possible Kildale finds mentioned above, another male burial was found in Wensley churchyard. This grave was also orientated east-west and contained a sword, spear and knife, and an iron sickle. These objects seem to symbolise the sources of Viking power and wealth, through force of arms (the weapons), through trade (the set of scales), and through agriculture (the sickle). In Ripon (North Yorkshire), 36 burials have been found associated with a two-celled church, the Ladykirk, which has produced sculptural fragments of eighth and ninth century date. Four burials within the chancel contained bone combs of a typical Anglo-Scandinavian type but it has also been suggested that these may represent priests, accompanied by liturgical equipment (Hall and Whyman 1996), rather than wavering pagans. As Halsall (2000) has pointed out, the presence of grave-goods in later first-millennium English burials has been enough for most researchers to label the occupant of the grave Viking, although many of the artefacts are Anglo-Saxon. In York, capital of the Viking kingdom, many years of excavation have produced less than half-a-dozen burials which have been identified as Scandinavians. Two accompanied skeletons were found immediately to the north of the present church of St Mary Bishophill Junior (Wenham *et al.* 1987). The first was of an adult male buried with an iron knife and a schist whetstone across his torso. He had a copper alloy buckle-plate at his waist, presumably from his belt, and was holding a St Peter's penny of *c.*905-15 in his hand. The second, of indeterminate sex, had a silver armring on the upper left arm. Several other bodies were buried with them on the same alignment, but these were unaccompanied by grave-goods, although several objects were found nearby, including a bone dress pin and fragmentary silver armlet. At the neighbouring church of St Mary Bishophill Senior there was a further possible Scandinavian grave with a tenth-century strap-end; a piece of Scandinavian silver appliqué ornament has been identified from the same site, probably from another burial (Hall 1997).

Apart from Repton, the evidence for accompanied burial in the graveyards of the southern Danelaw is very slight, and there is often nothing distinctively Scandinavian about many of the candidate burials. In Essex, there are two examples of Anglo-Saxon cemeteries in which there are accompanied burials. At Saffron Walden one burial in a row of Late Saxon graves contained a knife and a necklace with silver pendants which had probably been manufactured in Scandinavia in the tenth century. A copper alloy strap-end was also found on the site, and may have been disturbed from a second burial. There is a mention of a man being found buried with a horse from the same cemetery (Evison 1969). At Waltham Abbey a Middle Saxon cemetery with uncoffined burials also continued in use into the Viking period (Huggins 1988). One grave contained a decorated copper alloy plate of the late tenth or early eleventh century (Huggins 1984). At Sonning (Berkshire) the skeletons of two young males were discovered in 1966 during gravel quarrying. They were buried with a sword, a ring-headed pin, an Anglo-Saxon knife and six arrowheads (Evison 1969). Not far away, at Reading, a human skeleton had been found with a bent sword and a horse in 1831. At Santon Downham (Norfolk) an iron sword and pair of oval brooches were discovered in 1867 (Margeson 1997). They have been interpreted as representing a double burial of the late ninth century, but the brooches may represent an offering, like those at Claughton Hall. A pair of oval brooches, wired together, were also found at Bedale (North Yorkshire) (*plate 20*). The trefoil brooch from Low Dalby (North Yorkshire) may also have originated from a grave, although it was found on its own. In Nottingham two swords and a spear were found associated with two skulls; traces of wood were observed on the spear head, possibly representing a shield. Burial 451 from Middle Harling (Norfolk) contained four knives, a copper alloy buckle with iron plate, an iron buckle, a whetstone, a copper alloy earscoop, and an iron spur (Margeson 1997). Finally, there are a seaxe and knife from Wicken Fen (Cambridgeshire), although the knife is thought to be Anglo-Saxon (Evison 1969).

Nonetheless, it is most likely that Scandinavian settlers were using established cemeteries. The Vikings found a native population who were accustomed to burying their dead in communal cemeteries and appear to have quickly adopted this practice. From Scandinavia, the Nävelsjö stone, for example, records that 'Gurnkel set this stone in memory of Gunnar, his father, Rode's son. Helgi laid him, his brother, in a stone coffin in England in Bath'. It seems likely that Gunnar was buried in a Christian cemetery. Burial near a church, in holy ground, had been considered important for the aristocracy from the eighth century onwards, as attested by sculptural evidence, including elaborate grave covers such as those from Kirkdale (North Yorkshire), sarcophagi such as those from Bakewell and St Alkmund, Derby, and small inscribed upright grave markers such as those from York Minster. As the Minsters lost their control over burial, the growing number of manorial churches also acquired graveyards. As part of this process it seems that the Minster graveyards went out of use or contracted, and a number of cemeteries of early medieval religious communities have been discovered beyond the later churchyard walls. At Whitby (North Yorkshire) there was a pre-Conquest cemetery and probable enclosing ditch in the vicinity of Abbey Lands Farm, sealed by a thirteenth-century layer and overlain by ridge-and-furrow. At Aylesbury (Buckinghamshire), an ordered row cemetery of later eighth- to early tenth-century burials was found c.150m south-east of the medieval parish church of St Mary in an area which had, by Viking Age times, ceased to be used for burial, and where, by the twelfth and thirteenth centuries, rubbish pits indicate domestic activity. Similar sequences can be seen at Pontefract (West Yorkshire), Crayke (North Yorkshire), and Addingham (West Yorkshire). In the last case 55 graves were discovered in part of a cemetery which can be dated to the eighth to tenth centuries and which is to the west of the present parish churchyard. The cemetery appears to have gone out of use in the eleventh or twelfth century, when the manorial centre spread over the former burial ground, and burial was confined to an area much closer to the parish church (Adams 1996).

It is probable that the majority of English medieval churchyards were in use for burial before the Norman Conquest. Where there has been the opportunity for large scale churchyard excavation then accompanied burials have sometimes been found, as at Repton, but such cases appear to be unusual. At Wharram Percy, where establishment of the nucleated village may date to the Scandinavian settlement, and Scandinavian Borre style dress fittings have been recovered from the South Manor site, complete excavation of the church and associated cemetery has yielded no accompanied graves. Radiocarbon dating of the skeletons, however, has indicated that a large number date to the founding of the church, around the tenth century (*plate 19*).

At Raunds Furnells 363 burials have been excavated in a tenth- and eleventh-century graveyard clustered around the church within a rectangular ditched enclosure. It has been estimated that the graveyard probably served a community of around 40 individuals. Most of the bodies were simply placed in holes in the ground, although in about 60 per cent of cases slabs of limestone were used as head or foot pillows. There are indications of wooden coffins being used in a few cases and six elite burials were differentiated from the rest by being placed in lidded stone coffins. All the graves were aligned west-east with the head to the west. None were buried with grave-goods. The cemetery appears to have developed in rows and zones around the church, and post-holes may represent the position of grave-markers, although some graves may simply have been marked by shallow mounds. It was considered proper to bury infants in the cemetery; these were concentrated to the south and east of the church. After two centuries of use the Raunds churchyard was effectively full. In order to prepare it for its 'second generation' of burials there was dramatic clearance — posts and markers were uprooted; crosses and coffins were broken up; mounds levelled; hollows filled with mortar and sand from the demolition of the first church (Boddington 1996).

A striking feature of the various excavated burial grounds of the seventh to ninth centuries is the variety of burial practices and forms of commemoration. At Caister-by-Yarmouth

(Norfolk) an extensive cemetery has been excavated containing 12 burials that included clench nails (Darling and Gurney 1993). The cemetery is generally regarded as being Mid-Saxon, but some of the clench nail burials may be later. Developed Stamford ware was found in two graves, and a silver penny of Ecgbert of Wessex dated *c.*830-5 in another. Six of the burials with clench nails were of adult males; four were of adult females; one was an adolescent, and the last was of a child, aged 3-4 years. At Caister, in almost all cases the nails were spread over the body; only in one case were the timbers used as a bier. It appears, therefore, that re-used, lapped planks, possibly derived from boats, were being employed as grave-covers or coffin lids. At St Peter's Church, Barton-on-Humber, there were 16 graves with coffins of wood held together by clench nails; again these are seen as being boats, or parts of boats, used as coffins or covers (Rodwell and Rodwell 1982). Parts of old boats might have simply provided handy materials from which to construct coffins and biers in coastal and riverine regions, but this is really too mundane an explanation. Given the Scandinavian tradition of ship burial it is possible that the symbolism of the boats' timbers was significant, and that even those burials without grave-goods may be Scandinavian settlers, who may have accepted a Christian style burial but retained at least one element of their own customs. Similarly, at Thorpe-by-Norwich (Norfolk) at least two rows of clench nails were discovered with a burial beneath the former church. A Viking Age silver pin was also found, although apparently not with the burial.

The variety of burial rites is exposed most clearly by the excavations under York Minster (Philips and Heywood 1995). A cemetery was established on the site of the Roman basilica, beneath the south transept of the present Minster, in the early ninth century. Its limits were apparently defined by the bases of the outer walls of the old Roman headquarters building, and a Roman road which continued in use as a routeway. The Anglo-Saxon church probably lay to the south-west. Over 150 burials have been excavated, with roughly equal numbers of males and females. Less than 10 per cent of the burials were in coffins. One was in a lidded stone coffin with a recess for the head; up to six may have been in wooden coffins constructed of planks, and four were buried in wooden domestic storage chests, comprising one adult female, two adult males, one with a coin of 841-8, and an adolescent with traces of gold thread from a fine costume. There were also seven cist-type graves, including the use of pillow stones, and one corpse laid on a bed of mortar. Two of the bodies appear to have been placed upon wooden biers, rather than in coffins. The first was an adult male lying between two rows of clench nails which held together the oak planks of a wool-caulked clinker construction. Pillow stones had been positioned to support the head. This grave was also exceptional in that it was aligned east-west, unlike the others which followed the Roman building alignment. The second body laid on a bier was a child, aged 4-6. The rest of the York burials were simply placed in holes in the grounds, generally in oval-shaped cuts, without coffins or shrouds.

Twelve of the York burials were, however, placed on a bed of charcoal. They included both coffined and uncoffined burials. In just one case the charcoal had been laid over the body; otherwise the body was laid on the charcoal. These were not the latest burials and this must be seen as a particular custom reserved for a subset of burials. Charcoal burials are known from other cathedral cemeteries, including Exeter, Hereford, Oxford and Worcester, and appear to range in date from the ninth to the twelfth centuries. Charcoal may have served the practical function of soaking up fluids from a decaying corpse and avoiding unpleasant smells, but it seems to have been reserved for those of special status; perhaps it was thought to preserve the body from corruption. At Hereford all the burials inside the church were given a charcoal lining.

Twelve of the York Minster burials were marked by recumbent carved stone slabs (*plate 21*). A few had separate head- and/or foot-stones, including cut-down shafts, or fragments of earlier recumbent slabs. Most had a single recumbent slab decorated on the top only, including two of hogback form (see chapter 11). One adult male was buried under a re-used inscribed Roman memorial to which an Anglo-Saxon inscription had been added. These graves must certainly represent some of the elite of York who chose to be buried at their Minster church. It is impossible to say if they were Vikings or Anglo-Saxons, although several incorporate Scandinavian iconography, such as Sigurd and Wayland the Smith, indicating at least that Scandinavian influence had been absorbed (*plate 22*). Guthrith, one of the early Viking rulers of York, was buried in York Minster. One can say that at least two of the memorials marked the graves of children, aged 3-5 and 10-12, which is an interesting statement of how high status could be achieved in Viking York. Apparently some were born to it.

Cemeteries developed around all Saxon Cathedral churches and burials have been found during work on many sites, including Carlisle, Exeter, Gloucester, Hereford, London, North Elmham, Oxford, Shrewsbury, Winchester and Worcester, as well as York. Their use as burial places probably followed from their function as shrines and resting places for the bodies or relics of holy saints. Those seeking salvation hoped to benefit by being buried in proximity to a holy relic. At North Elmham 194 eleventh-century graves were excavated within a fenced enclosure. All were aligned west-east with their heads in the west. There was no clear evidence of coffins, no trace of grave-markers, and no grave-goods. At the Castle Green, Hereford, 87 burials were excavated from a much larger cemetery dating from the seventh to the twelfth centuries. The burials were initially around a timber church which was replaced by a stone structure in the eleventh century. The method of corpse disposal appears to have been particularly important in the ninth and tenth centuries: of 18 burials, 13 were in charcoal, 12 in coffins, and 4 had pillow stones (Shoesmith 1980).

In summary, the apparent shortage of obvious Scandinavian style burials over much of the Danelaw has to be set against the variety of new burial rites, including the use of commemorative monuments (chapter 11). As Anglo-Saxon and Viking cultures came into contact, new identities were forged. In some cases, such as the north-west and in specific circumstances elsewhere (such as Heath Wood), these comprised the maintenance and even development of a distinctive Viking identity. Elsewhere it was expedient for the newcomers to align themselves with existing elite practices, or to invent new ones.

From the burial evidence it appears that the new identity frequently included adoption of Christianity. Haraldr Bluetooth claimed that he was the first to make the Danes Christian, sometime in the second half of the tenth century. If this was indeed the start of a top-down process, whereby kings encouraged their subjects to take up new religions, then those Danes settling in England a hundred years earlier would have arrived as pagans. Norway and Sweden were each converted to Christianity later than Denmark; and the strength of paganism amongst the Hiberno-Norse may be reflected in the accompanied burials of the Irish Sea area, and north-west England. Elsewhere Viking leaders may have considered it politic to abandon pagan practices in order to win favour with the native population. Guthrum agreed to be baptised in order to make peace with Ælfred, after having been defeated by him at the Battle of Eddington. Pagan merchants undertook baptism in order to do business with their Christian counterparts. Pagan settlers were baptised in order to take Christian English wives.

Scandinavian settlers were particularly adaptable to local circumstances, and so was their religion. Paganism was not an organised religion like Christianity. The Pantheon was sufficiently flexible to admit the Christian God, especially since Anglo-Saxon writers endowed Christ with heroic qualities. As we shall see in the next chapter, memorial crosses bearing combinations of pagan and Christian motifs appear in northern England from the mid-tenth century, and Scandinavian settlers began to build churches. Yet the stone sculpture suggests that the conversion was just a little pragmatic and not altogether complete. As late as the reign of Knutr it was felt necessary to condemn the activities of wizards and to forbid the worship of 'idols, heathen gods, the sun or moon, fire or flood, springs, and stones or any kind of woodland tree'. Many present-day folk practices still contain fragments of pagan ceremonies, perhaps still preserving today Scandinavian rituals which once existed.

11

MONUMENTS IN STONE

One of the most durable forms of evidence of Viking Age England are the Anglo-Scandinavian stone monuments which can be found in many churches and churchyards, especially in Derbyshire, Lincolnshire, Yorkshire, Lancashire and Cumbria. Yet whilst the animal ornament and iconography is in a Scandinavian style, the erection of stone crosses was not a Scandinavian tradition.

Viking Age sculpture represents a special blend of Scandinavian, Anglo-Saxon and Celtic traditions. Although rune-stone memorials were erected in several parts of Scandinavia, and Gotland is famous for its picture-stones, there were no stone carvings in Scandinavia until the end of the tenth century. In England, however, there was a flourishing Anglo-Saxon tradition of stone sculpture. Elaborately decorated architectural stonework and standing stone crosses are found at early monastic sites (Lang 1988). Many crosses may have been grave-markers but some appear to have been memorials to saints, or boundary markers. Stone sarcophagi and decorated recumbent stone slabs were also sometimes used to mark particularly wealthy graves.

Scandinavian settlers in the Danelaw embraced the Christian tradition of erecting stone memorials to the dead and developed it as their own. Anglo-Scandinavian crosses are particularly prevalent at sites where there was already Anglo-Saxon sculpture, suggesting less disruption to ecclesiastical sites than is often assumed. At the monastery church at Lastingham (North Yorkshire), the crypt contains sculpture decorated in both Anglo-Saxon and Anglo-Scandinavian styles. It has been estimated that 60 per cent of Yorkshire sites with Anglo-Saxon sculpture also have Anglo-Scandinavian sculpture; in Cumbria, of 15 sites with Anglo-Saxon sculpture, 12 also have Anglo-Scandinavian crosses. The patrons may have changed but it appears the local masons still found employment. Some continuity is also apparent in the styles of ornament used. Although Anglo-Scandinavian sculpture borrows decorative styles and motifs that can be found throughout the Viking world, there are also Anglo-Saxon elements in the design. The vine scrolls at Middleton, Brompton and Leeds, for example, are clearly derived from those on the earlier Anglo-Saxon crosses at Ruthwell and Bewcastle. The organisation of decoration into distinct panels was also an Anglo-Saxon practice rather than a Scandinavian stylistic trait.

However, by the Viking Age, stone memorials are found at five times as many places as in the eighth and ninth centuries. In Cumbria there are 115 monuments of the tenth and eleventh centuries from 36 sites. In Yorkshire there are approximately 500 monuments at over 100 locations, about 80 per cent of which may be dated to the Viking

Age. Some are concentrated at known religious centres but Anglo-Scandinavian sculpture has also been identified at numerous sites where there is no Anglo-Saxon work. These sites represent an expansion in the number of centres commissioning crosses from the tenth century onwards. This increase corresponds with the decline of monastic patronage, and the transfer of resources to a new secular aristocracy. These were prosperous landholders, particularly those farming the rich agricultural land of the Vales of York and Pickering. Christian crosses now came under secular influence as the new local elite employed them to signify their status and their allegiances.

Tenth-century sculpture in the Danelaw is therefore different from the sculpture that preceded it, not only in terms of ornamentation, but also in terms of location and function, since much more is clearly funerary. These monuments represent individual aristocratic burials. At most churches in Lincolnshire and Yorkshire there is sculpture from only one or two monuments, and David Stocker has suggested that many of these crosses were the founding monuments in a new generation of parochial graveyards. However, there are a number of churches with many more sculptures. These are frequently located in trading places, such as Marton-on-Trent, Bicker and St Mark's and St Mary-le-Wigford, in what has been termed the 'strand' of Lincoln (Stocker 2000). These exceptional graveyards may belong to unusual settlements occupied primarily by mercantile elites.

In Ryedale, where most Anglo-Saxon churches contain Anglo-Scandinavian crosses, these include a distinct group of so-called warrior crosses, such as those at Levisham, Weston, Sockburn, and Middleton (North Yorkshire). The Middleton

17 *The Middleton Cross was extracted from the church fabric in 1948. It was once thought to represent a Viking warrior lying in his grave but is now generally interpreted as a warrior-lord sitting on his gift-stool or throne. The pellets above his shoulders are part of the chair. He is wearing a pointed helmet and carries a long knife, or scramasax, at his belt. He is surrounded by his symbols of power, including spear, sword, axe and shield.*

warrior was once thought to represent a pagan Viking warrior lying in his grave, but is now seen as an Anglo-Scandinavian lord seated on his gift-stool or throne and surrounded by his symbols of power (*17*). Regional patterns in ornamentation, form and iconography, as well as reflecting locations of schools of sculptural production, may also reflect regional power groups, in which lords signalled their allegiances and status through commissioning particular types of sculpture. A uniformity of style and ornament can be identified across the whole of eighth-century Anglo-Saxon Northumbria, maintained by a common monastic tradition and inter-monastic contact. This was broken down in the ninth and tenth centuries after the Viking immigration, with the development of identifiable local sculptural traditions and workshops (see chapter 7).

In the coastal areas of north-west Cumbria, for example, there is a concentration of circle-headed crosses. The distribution is centred on the Viking colonies of the western seaboard between Anglesey and northern Cumbria and illustrates the importance of coastal links. An outlier at Gargrave (North Yorkshire) suggests that settlers in the upper river valleys may have originated from the west rather than the east.

In Yorkshire, the grave slabs excavated at York Minster served as a model for many Yorkshire stone monuments, although the motifs were borrowed and modified in Ryedale and other areas. In Ryedale, for instance, the crosses at Kirkbymoorside, Middleton and Levisham all share the same peculiar style of cross head, with a raised outer crest on a ring connecting the arms. The sculptors frequently combined new with old elements. In York the tenth-century sculptors promoted original Anglo-Scandinavian-style designs as well as maintaining continuity with Anglian traditions. Most of the Yorkshire crosses were probably carved not in the initial phase of Scandinavian settlement, but in the period 900-50, after the expulsion of the Norse from Dublin, during the period in which Yorkshire was under strong Hiberno-Norse influence (Lang 1978; 1991). After the expulsion of Erik Bloodaxe in 954, York metropolitan sculpture developed more under Mercian influence, while Ryedale sculpture became introverted and insular with little evidence for further external influence (Walsh 1994).

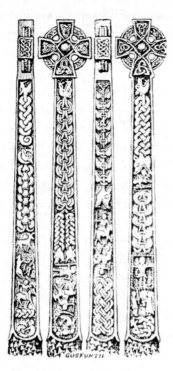

18 The Gosforth Cross, Cumbria (after Collingwood). The cross, which stands 4.2m (14ft) high, was cut from a single piece of red sandstone. Its pictures exploit the links and contrasts between Scandinavian and Christian theology. On one side there is a Crucifixion scene in which Mary Magdalene appears dressed as a Valkyrie, with a trailing dress and long pigtail. On the other sides scenes from Ragnarok are depicted, at the moment when the gods' enemies, the forces of evil, break loose from their restraining bonds. The Fenris wolf is seen escaping from his bonds to attack Odin. The evil god Loki is seen chained beneath a venomous serpent whilst his wife catches poison in a cup. Heimdal, watchman of the gods, is also depicted with his spear and horn. In the ensuing battle monsters and gods perish as earthquake and fire sweep all away. From this chaos emerges a new cleansed world

In Lincolnshire the tenth-century sculpture also represents the remains of grave markers set up to commemorate the founding burials in a new generation of parish graveyards (Everson and Stocker 1999). This new burial fashion reaches Lincolnshire slightly later than Yorkshire; all the crosses were erected between 930-1030, and most can be dated 950-1000. These are again derived from Hiberno-Norse prototypes in Yorkshire, north-west England and the Isle of Man.

In the Peak District area of Derbyshire, Anglian origins of the sculptural tradition are again reflected in the use of round shafts to the crosses. The majority of the Derbyshire crosses have been dated between 910-50. They demonstrate an Anglo-Scandinavian domination of political landscape, but it has been suggested that the level of continuity of design also indicates an acceptance of the West Saxon overlord and his Church (Sidebottom 2000).

Outside the Danelaw there are fewer examples of Viking Age sculpture, although examples from St Oswald's Priory (Gloucester), Ramsbury (Wiltshire) and Bibury (Gloucester-shire) do indicate the spread of Scandinavian taste into southern England in the tenth and eleventh centuries. In Cornwall, Scandinavian motifs appear occasionally, such as at Sancreed, Temple Moor, Padstow and Cardynham, displaying links with the Irish Sea area. The Isle of Man has one of the greatest concentrations of Viking Age sculpture, with 48 crosses produced in a relatively short time span of *c.*930-1020.

ICONOGRAPHY

The iconography of the Scandinavian crosses illustrates the close links of the Irish Sea area in the Viking Age (Bailey 1980). The same motifs and stories are frequently depicted in the Isle of Man and Yorkshire. The ring chain ornament seen on Gautr's cross on the Isle of Man, for example, is also found in Cumbria, Northumbria and North Wales. Other Manx motifs, such as a distinctive style of knotwork tendril, display links with Yorkshire, particularly Barwick-in-Elmet and Spofforth, and there are further similarities with crosses in Aberford, Collingham, Saxton, and Sinnington all suggesting a great deal of contact and movement between the Isle of

Man and Yorkshire (Walsh 1994). The hart-and-hound motif is found on the Isle of Man and in Cumbria, Lancashire and Yorkshire. The bound devil depicted at Kirkby Stephen (Cumbria) has parallels in similar figures from Maughold on the Isle of Man. The legend of Sigurd is also a popular scene in both areas, suggesting a shared set of beliefs and traditions.

Although most monuments are purely Christian, with the Crucifixion being the most popular scene, Christian, pagan and secular subjects are all depicted. In many cases Christian and pagan stories are combined by the sculptor, giving a Christian twist to a pagan tradition. One of the most startling examples is the Gosforth Cross (*18*) which has the Crucifixion depicted on one side whilst scenes from Ragnorok are shown on the others. The popularity of Sigurd on many crosses stems from his use to honour the dead, but Sigurd's struggle with the dragon Fafnir also provides a link with heroic Christian themes. On a grave slab from York Minster (*plate 22*) Sigurd is depicted poised to stab the dragon. A panel from the cross at Nunburnholme (East Yorkshire) in which Sigurd has been recarved over a Eucharistic scene may be drawing attention to the Sigurd feast as a pagan version of the Eucharist. The heroic figure Weland, the flying smith, is another popular theme with subtle ambiguities. At Leeds (West Yorkshire) he is related to angels, and the eagle of St John.

Burial customs indicate that Scandinavian settlers apparently assimilated Christian ideas quite rapidly (chapter 10). Scandinavian paganism embraced a broad pantheon of gods, each of which had particular characteristics and might be called upon for specific functions; perhaps the Christian God was one more to be adopted into the fold. At Gosforth pagan and Christian images may have been seen as equivalent by the craftsman, rather than as the triumph of the new over the old; perhaps they were even regarded as aspects of the same theme.

HOGBACKS

A particularly distinctive form of Viking Age funerary monument is the so-called hogback tomb, named after its arched form. Hogbacks are recumbent stone monuments, generally about 1.5m in length. They are basically the shape of a bow-sided building with a ridged roof and curved side walls and are often decorated with architectural features such as shingle roofs, and stylised wattle walls. Over 50 hogbacks are also decorated with end-beasts (*plate 23*). These are generally bear-like creatures, although wolves or dogs are also known; sometimes they are shown with two legs, sometimes with four; many are clearly muzzled.

The distribution of hogbacks is mainly restricted to northern England and central Scotland, with a few outliers (*19*). They are concentrated especially in North Yorkshire and Cumbria, with none in the Isle of Man, and only single examples in Wales and Ireland. There are no hogbacks in the Danelaw areas of Lincolnshire and East Anglia and their distribution appears to be restricted to those areas which also have Hiberno-Norse and Norse place-names. Thus hogbacks appear to have developed in those areas which were subject to Hiberno-Norse influence, although they clearly spread east of the Pennines. Their absence from the Isle of Man may be explained simply as a function of the local geology, as the Manx slate would be difficult to cut into substantial three-dimensional

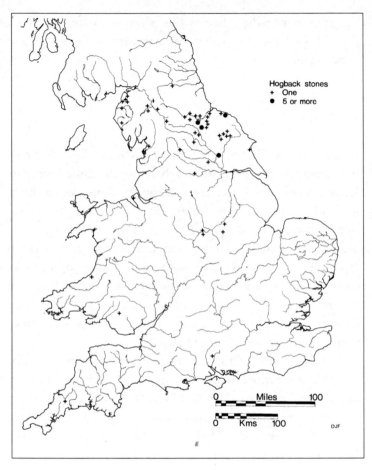

Hogback stones
+ One
● 5 or more

0   Miles   100

0   Kms   100

DJF

19 Map of hogback tombstones (after Lang 1984)

forms, being more appropriate to flat slabs. Three Cornish hogbacks from Lanivet, St Tudy and St Buryan demonstrate the long-distance contacts of the Norse. This coastal distribution pattern is also seen around Scotland, emphasizing the coastal nature of much of Norse settlement.

It is likely that hogbacks are a tenth-century phenomenon; it has been suggested that most were carved within the period 920-70 (Lang 1984). Like most of the Anglo-Scandinavian sculpture in England, therefore, they belong not to the initial phase of Scandinavian colonisation in the ninth century, but to a second wave of Hiberno-Norse immigrants. Their origin has been much debated as they have no clear ancestors, either in Britain or Scandinavia. The best parallels are house-shaped shrines. In Anglo-Saxon England, stone shrines were used to contain or cover the body of a saint, although no 'shrine-tombs' are known from the area of hogbacks. Recumbent grave slabs were used to mark important burials and the Viking Age grave slabs excavated from under York Minster have central ridges. Perhaps hogbacks should be seen as three-dimensional extensions of this idea. Certainly they combine a number of cultural elements, including Trelleborg style bow-sided halls, Anglo-Saxon shrines and animal ornament. Some may have formed part of composite monuments with cross shafts at the ends, in the same way that some of the York Minster grave-slabs have end-stones. The so-called Giant's Grave at Penrith combines a hogback stone with cross shafts in this fashion, although the possibility remains that this is a later rearrangement of the stones. The end-beasts may have originated as animals carved on separate end-stones which have subsequently been combined in a single three-dimensional monument. David Stocker has suggested that the significance of the muzzled bear may have been as the Christian symbol of a mother bear licking her cubs and bringing them to life (Stocker 2000).

Most hogbacks are no longer in their original location and so there are few cases where they can be associated with burials, although in the excavations under York Minster two hogback stones were found over burials. It has also been suggested that the spearhead found in Heysham churchyard may have come from the hogback burial (chapter 10). To the east of the Old Minster, Winchester, there was a group of four graves with limestone covers. One of these, grave 119, was covered with a hogback stone. This was the burial of a man of about 23, buried in a wooden coffin, his head resting on a pillow of flint and limestone; a Roman coin had been placed in the coffin. The hogback carried an Old English inscription along its back: 'Here lies Gunni, Eorl's [or the earl's] fellow'. Subsequently, an inscription in Danish runes has been discovered on a fragment of stone found built into St Maurices's church tower. Both are likely to have been early eleventh-century memorials, possibly commemorating followers of Knutr (Kjølbye-Biddle and Page 1975).

RUNES

The use of runic inscriptions is uncommon in England but is a feature of the Viking Age sculpture of the Isle of Man (Page 1987; 1999). Runic alphabets were developed by various Germanic and Scandinavian peoples in northern Europe in the first millennium AD. They continued in use into the medieval period but always seem to have been reserved for particular functions, such as formal inscriptions. In England a few Anglo-Saxon crosses, such as those at Collingham (West Yorkshire) and Hackness (North Yorkshire), were inscribed with Old English runes.

Some runes appear to have been endowed with magical properties, and weapons may have been inscribed to give them special powers. The runic script is particularly well suited, however, to being inscribed on wood and stone, the characters being formed of combinations of diagonal and vertical strokes. In some areas of Viking Age Scandinavia it became common practice to erect commemorative rune stones to honour the dead. They sometimes mark the grave but frequently they commemorate the death of someone far from home. Often they were erected at the roadside or at bridging points or meeting places. In Norway today there are some 40 rune stones; in Denmark less than 200; and in Sweden some 3500. The practice was not, however, generally followed in Scandinavian settlements overseas. There are no rune stones from Normandy, none in Iceland, two from the Faroes, and only a handful from Ireland. About half a dozen have been found in Scotland, with similar numbers from Orkney and Shetland.

In Britain the tradition was only developed on the Isle of Man, where the largest collection of runes in the British Isles is to be found inscribed on the stone crosses. The Scandinavians who settled in England did not generally maintain this custom and Viking runic finds are rare. Apart from the Winchester rune stone (above) the only other runic memorial in England was discovered in 1852 during excavation for a warehouse on the south side of St Paul's Cathedral (*plate 36*). It is likely that this eleventh-century stone was in its original position marking a grave, as the remains of a skeleton were found immediately to the north of the slab. Along one edge of the stone was the inscription 'Ginna and Toki had this stone set up', probably to commemorate a Danish or Swedish follower of Knutr. Ginna may have been his widow and Toki his son; the name of the dead man was perhaps on another slab, never found.

The only other Danish runes from England are casual graffiti: inscriptions on animal bones from eleventh-century butcher's waste from St Albans, and a comb case from Lincoln. On the other hand, Norse runes continued in use for some time in the north of England. There are runic graffiti from Carlisle Cathedral, Dearham (Cumbria) and Settle (North Yorkshire), and late eleventh and twelfth-century inscriptions on a sundial from Skelton-in-Cleveland, and on a font from Bridekirk (Cumbria). An inscription from Pennington (Cumbria) records the builder and mason of the church in bastardised Norse.

ANGLO–SCANDINAVIAN IDENTITIES

In summary, Viking Age stone sculpture represents the invention of new cultural traditions which developed at the interface between Anglo-Saxon, Celtic and Scandinavian peoples. These memorials symbolised identity and power, combining Christian traditions with the needs of the secular aristocracy. In Anglo-Saxon England, monasteries were centres of power and wealth, and the standing crosses would have been recognised as symbols of authority. It was natural, therefore, for the new local elites who came to power as a result of Viking incursions to seek to express their own power through the erection of stone monuments in Scandinavian art styles. Those patrons who commissioned crosses, such as that at Gosforth, supported craftsmen who drew extensively upon local traditions, but added motifs from pagan iconography. It should not be surprising that those areas where former large estates were being broken up into smaller land units under private ownership often coincide with a high density of sculpture. It was in these places where there were new claims to land which required representation in solid stone monuments which invoked the power of the Church, as well as the sword.

Viking Age England was a melting pot of cultural traditions. In all aspects of society, from settlement patterns to industrial production, it has been shown that for over 250 years England was subject to rapid and far-reaching changes. One of the questions posed at the start of this book was to ask how far the Vikings were responsible for this. In many aspects of life they had a catalytic role, but it is rather simplistic just to speak of Anglo-Saxons and Vikings. Over the course of the Viking Age new identities were being forged, and language and customs were each used to define and articulate an Anglo-Scandinavian identity. Whether it was through new place-names and new words, new forms of burial, new building types, or simply new dress fashion accessories, the peoples of Viking Age England were constantly re-inventing themselves. This process continues to the present day where, as the inhabitants of England continue to redefine their relationship with each other and with the peoples of continental Europe and Scandinavia, it is as relevant as ever.

FURTHER READING

I THE VIKING AGE

Amongst the best general overviews of the Viking Age are:
J. Graham-Campbell (ed) *Cultural Atlas of the Viking World* (Abingdon
    1994)
H. Loyn *The Vikings in Britain* (Oxford 1994)
E. Roesdahl *et al. The Vikings in England* (London 1981)
E. Roesdahl *The Vikings* (London 1991)
P. Sawyer (ed) *The Oxford Illustrated History of the Vikings* (Oxford
    1997)

*Scotland, Wales and the Isle of Man are outside the scope of this book; for
recent surveys of Scandinavian settlement in these areas see:*
B.E. Crawford *Scandinavian Scotland* (Leicester 1987)
W. Davies *Wales in the Early Middle Ages* (Leicester 1982)
C. Fell *et al.* (eds.) *The Viking Age in the Isle of Man* (London 1983)
R.A. Hall *Viking Age Archaeology in Britain and Ireland* (Princes
    Risborough 1990)
O. Owen *The Sea Road: A Viking Voyage through Scotland* (Edinburgh
    1999)
J.D. Richards 'Scandinavian Britain' in J. Hunter and I. Ralston (eds.)
    The Archaeology of Britain (London 1999), 194-209

Further reading

A. Ritchie *Viking Scotland* (London 1993)

C.E. Batey and J. Graham-Campbell *Vikings in Scotland: An Archaeological Survey* (Edinburgh 1998)

For issues of definition of Vikings and the Viking Age see:

M.P. Evison 'All in the genes? Evaluating the biological evidence of contact and migration' in D. Hadley and J.D. Richards (eds.), 2000, 277-94

C. Fell 'Old English *wicing*: a question of semantics' *Proc Brit Acad* 72 (1986) 295-316

C. Fell 'Modern English Viking' in T. Turville-Petre and M. Gelling (eds.) *Studies in Honour of Kenneth Cameron*, Leeds Studies in English, New Series 18 (1987) 111-22

D. Hadley ' "And they proceeded to plough and to support themselves": the Scandinavian Settlement of England', *Anglo-Norman Studies* 19 (1997) 69-96

D. Hadley and J.D. Richards (eds) *Cultures in contact: Scandinavian settlement in England in the ninth and tenth centuries* (York 2000)

M. Innes 'Danelaw identities: ethnicity, regionalism and political allegiance', in D. Hadley and J.D. Richards (eds.), 2000, 65-88

M. Müller-Wille 'The political misuse of Scandinavian prehistory in the years 1933-1945' in E. Roesdahl and P.M. Sørensen (eds) *The Waking of Angantyr* (Århus 1996) 156-75

B. Myhre 'The beginning of the Viking Age – some current archaeological problems' in A. Faulkes and R. Perkins (eds) *Viking revaluations* (London 1993), 182-204

B. Myrhe 'The archaeology of the early Viking Age in Norway' in H.B. Clarke, M. Ní Mhaonaigh and R.Ó. Floinn (eds.) *Ireland and Scandinavia in the Early Viking Age* (Dublin 1998), 3-36

S. Trafford 'Ethnicity, migration theory and the historiography of the Scandinavian settlement of England' in D. Hadley and J.D. Richards (eds.), 2000, 17-39

A. Wawn *The Vikings and the Victorians: inventing the old north in nineteenth-century Britain* (Cambridge 2000)

D.M. Wilson 'The Viking Age in British literature and history in the eighteenth and nineteenth centuries' in E. Roesdahl and P.M. Sørensen (eds.) *The Waking of Angantyr* (Århus 1996) 58-71

2 VIKING RAIDS

E. Bakka 'Some English decorated metal objects found in Norwegian graves', *Arbok for universitetet i Bergen, humanistisk serie*, I, 1963

M. Biddle and B. Kjølbye-Biddle 'Repton and the Vikings', *Antiquity* 66 (1992) 36-51

M.A.S. Blackburn and H. Pagan 'A revised check-list of coin hoards from the British Isles, c.500-1100', in M.A.S. Blackburn (ed.), *Anglo-Saxon monetary history: essays in memory of Michael Dolley* (Leicester 1986) 291-313

N.P. Brooks and J. Graham-Campbell 'Reflections on the Viking-Age silver hoard from Croydon, Surrey', in M.A.S. Blackburn (ed.), *Anglo-Saxon monetary history: essays in memory of Michael Dolley* (Leicester 1986) 91-110

J. Dent 'Skerne', *Current Archaeology* 91 (1984) 251-3

J. Dyer 'Earthworks of the Danelaw frontier', in P.J. Fowler (ed.), *Archaeology and the landscape* (London 1972) 222-36

B.J.N. Edwards 'Viking silver ingots from Bowes Moor, Yorkshire', *Antiq J* 65 (1985) 457-9

J. Graham-Campbell 'Anglo-Scandinavian equestrian equipment in eleventh-century England', *Anglo-Norman Studies* 14 (1992) 77-89

J. Graham-Campbell (ed) *Viking treasure from the north west: the Cuerdale hoard in its context,* National Museums and Galleries of Merseyside Occasional Papers 5 (Liverpool 1992)

H. St G. Gray 'Trial excavations in the so-called "Danish camp" at Warham', *Antiq J* 13 (1933) 399-413

S.B.F. Jansson *Swedish Vikings in England, the evidence of the rune stones* (London 1966)

S.B.F. Jansson *Runes in Sweden* (Sweden 1990)

S. Keynes 'The Vikings in England, c.790-1016', in P. Sawyer (ed.), *The Oxford Illustrated History of the Vikings* (Oxford 1997), 48-82

S. Kruse 'Ingots and weight units in Viking Age silver hoards', *World Archaeology* 20 (1980) 285-301

P.H. Sawyer *The Age of the Vikings* (London 1971), second edition

W.A. Seaby and P. Woodfield 'Viking stirrups from England and their background', *Medieval Archaeology* 24 (1980) 87-122

D.M. Wilson 'Some neglected late Anglo-Saxon swords', *Medieval Archaeology* 9 (1965) 32-54

3 VIKING COLONISATION

Settlement patterns

D. Hadley 'Multiple estates and the origins of the manorial structure
of the northern Danelaw', *J Hist Geography* 22 (1996) 3-15

D. Hadley 'And they proceeded to plough and to support themselves',
Anglo-Norman Studies 19 (1997) 69-96

G.R.J. Jones 'Early territorial organization in northern England and
its bearing on the Scandinavian settlement', in A. Small (ed.) *The
Fourth Viking Congress* (Edinburgh 1965), 67-84

T. Unwin 'Towards a model of Anglo-Scandinavian rural settlement
in England' in D. Hooke (ed.), *Anglo-Saxon settlements* (Oxford
1988) 77-98

Place-names and linguistic evidence

K. Cameron 'The Scandinavians in Derbyshire: the place-name
evidence', *Nottingham Medieval Studies* 2 (1958) 86-118

K. Cameron *Scandinavian settlement in the territory of the Five Boroughs:
The place-name evidence* (Nottingham 1965)

K. Cameron 'Scandinavian settlement in the territory of the Five
Boroughs: the place-name evidence part II: place-names in Thorp',
Medieval Scandinavia 3 (1970) 35-49

K. Cameron 'Scandinavian settlement in the territory of the Five
Boroughs: the place-name evidence part III: the Grimston-
Hybrids', in P. Clemoes and K. Hughes (eds) *England before the
Conquest* (Cambridge 1971), 147-63

E. Ekwall 'How long did the Scandinavian language survive in
England?' in N. Bøgholm, A. Brusendorff and C.A. Bodelsen (eds.)
*A Grammatical Miscellany offerred to Otto Jespersen on his seventieth
birthday* (London 1930), 17-30

G. Fellows-Jensen 'Scandinavian personal names in Lincolnshire and
Yorkshire', *Navnestudier* 7 (Copenhagen 1968)

G. Fellows-Jensen 'Scandinavian settlement names in Yorkshire',
Navnestudier 11 (Copenhagen 1972)

G. Fellows-Jensen 'The Vikings in England: a review', *Anglo-Saxon
England* 4 (1975) 181-206

G. Fellows-Jensen *Scandinavian settlement names in the East Midlands*
(Copenhagen 1978)

G. Fellows-Jensen *Scandinavian settlement names in the North-West* (Copenhagen 1985)

G. Fellows-Jensen 'Danish place-names and personal names in England: the influence of Cnut?' in A. Rumble (ed.) *The Reign of Cnut* (London 1994), 125-40

J. Hines 'Scandinavian English: a creole in context', in P. Sture Ureland and G. Broderick (eds) *Language Contact in the British Isles* (Tübingen 1991), 403-27

J. Insley *Scandinavian personal names in Norfolk* (Uppsala 1994)

R.I. Page 'How long did the Scandinavian language survive in England? The epigraphical evidence', in P. Clemoes and K. Hughes (eds) *England before the Conquest* (Cambridge 1971), 165-81

V. Smart 'Scandinavians, Celts, and Germans in Anglo-Saxon England: the evidence of moneyers' names', in M.A.S. Blackburn (ed.), *Anglo-Saxon monetary history: Essays in memory of Michael Dolley* (Leciester1986) 171-84

M. Townend 'Viking Age England as a bilingual society' in D. Hadley and J.D. Richards (eds.), 2000, 89-105

Regional studies

J.R. Baldwin and R.D. Whyte (eds.) *The Scandinavians in Cumbria* (Edinburgh 1985)

P. Drewett, D. Rudling and M. Gardiner *The South East to AD 1000* (London 1988)

M. Gelling *The West Midlands in the Early Middle Ages* (Leicester 1992)

N.J. Higham *The Northern Counties to AD 1000* (London 1986)

C.D. Morris 'Northumbria and the Viking settlement: the evidence for land-holding', *Archaeologia Aeliana*, 5 ser, 5 (1977) 81-103

C.D. Morris 'Viking and native in northern England: A case-study', *Proc Eighth Viking Congress* (Odense 1981) 223-44

C.D. Morris 'The Vikings in the British Isles: some aspects of their settlement and economy', in R.T. Farrell (ed.) *The Vikings* (Chichester 1982), 70-94

P.H. Sawyer *Anglo-Saxon Lincolnshire* (Lincoln 1998)

P. Stafford *The East Midlands in the Early Middle Ages* (Leicester 1985)

M. Todd *The South-West to AD 1000* (London 1987)

B. Yorke *Wessex in the Early Middle Ages* (Leicester 1995)

Sites and settlements

P.V. Addyman 'Late Saxon settlements in the St Neots area: II. The Little Paxton settlement and enclosures', *Proc Cambridge Antiq Soc* 62 (1969) 59–93

P.V. Addyman 'Late Saxon settlements in the St. Neots area: III. The village or township at St Neots', *Proc Cambridge Antiq Soc* 64 (1972) 45–99

R.A. Adkins and M.R. Petchey 'Secklow Hundred Mound and other meeting place mounds in England' *Archaeol J* 141 (1984) 243–51

G. Beresford 'Tresmorn. St Gennys', *Cornish Archaeology* 10 (1971) 55–73

G. Beresford 'Three deserted medieval settlements on Dartmoor', *Medieval Archaeology* 23 (1979) 98–158

G. Beresford 'Goltho: the development of an early medieval manor c.850–1150', *English Heritage Archaeol Report* 4 (London 1987)

M. Beresford and J.G. Hurst *Wharram Percy: Deserted Medieval Village* (London 1990)

J. Blair 'Palaces or minsters? Northampton and Cheddar reconsidered' *Anglo-Saxon England* 25 (1996) 97–121

R. Bruce-Mitford Mawgan 'Porth: a settlement of the late Saxon period on the north Cornish coast' *English Heritage Archaeol Report* 13 (London 1997)

D.G. Buckley and J.D. Hedges 'The Bronze Age and Saxon settlements at Springfield Lyons, Essex: An interim report', *Essex County Council Occ Paper* 5 (Chelmsford 1987)

G. Cadman and G. Foard 'Raunds: manorial and village origins', in M. Faull (ed.), 1984, 81–100

D. Coggins, K.J. Fairless and C.E. Batey 'Simy Folds: An early medieval settlement in Upper Teesdale, Co Durham', *Medieval Archaeology* 27 (1983) 1–26

B. Cunliffe 'Excavations at Portchester Castle. Volume II: Saxon' *Soc Antiq Res Rep* 33 (London 1976)

B.K. Davison 'Excavations at Sulgrave, Northamptonshire, 1968', *Archaeol J* 125 (1968) 305–7

S. Dickinson 'Bryant's Gill, Kentmere: Another "Viking-Period" Ribblehead?', in J.R. Baldwin and I.D. Whyte (eds.), *The Scandinavians in Cumbria* (Edinburgh 1985) 83–8

D. Dudley and E.M. Minter 'Excavation of a medieval settlement at Treworld', *Cornish Archaeology* 5 (1966) 34–58

J.R. Fairbrother 'Faccombe Netherton. Excavations of a Saxon and Medieval manorial complex' *British Museum Occ Paper* 74 (London 1990)

G. Foard and T. Pearson 'The Raunds area project: first interim report', *Northamptonshire Archaeology* 20 (1985) 3-21

M. Gardiner 'The excavation of a Late Anglo-Saxon settlement at Market Field, Steyning, 1988-89' *Sussex Archaeol Coll* 131 (1993) 21-67

M. Gardiner and C. Greatorex 'Archaeological excavations in Steyning, 1992-95: further evidence for the evolution of a Late Saxon small town' *Sussex Archaeol Coll* 135 (1997) 143-71

J.G. Hurst 'The Wharram Research Project: Results to 1983', *Medieval Archaeology* 28 (1984) 77-111

A. King 'Gauber high pasture, Ribblehead — an interim report', in R.A. Hall (ed.), *Viking Age York and the North CBA Res Rep* 27 (London 1978) 21-5

S. Losco-Bradley and H.M. Wheeler 'Anglo-Saxon Settlement in the Trent Valley: Some aspects', in M. Faull (ed.), *Studies in Late Anglo-Saxon Settlement* (Oxford 1984) 101-14

D. O'Sullivan and R. Young Lindisfarne: *Holy Island* (London 1995)

P. Rahtz *The Saxon and Medieval Palaces at Cheddar Brit Archaeol Rep, (Brit Ser)*, 65 (Oxford 1979)

A. Reynolds *Later Anglo-Saxon England* (Stroud 1999)

J.D. Richards 'Cottam: An Anglian and Anglo-Scandinavian settlement on the Yorkshire Wolds' *Archaeol J* 156 (1999) 1-110

P. Stamper and R. Croft 'Wharram: A Study of Settlement in the Yorkshire Wolds VIII: The South Manor' *York University Archaeological Publications* 10 (2000)

P. Wade-Martins 'Excavations in North Elmham Park 1967-1972', *East Anglian Archaeology* 9 (1980)

4 THE GROWTH OF TOWNS

L. Alcock *Cadbury Castle, Somerset. The Early Medieval Archaeology* (Cardiff 1995)

P. Andrews (ed.) *Excavations at Hamwic: Volume 2: excavations at Six Dials* (York 1997)

M. Atkin 'The Anglo-Saxon urban landscape in East Anglia', *Landscape Hist* 7 (1985) 27-40

T. Austin 'Viking-period Chester. An alternative perspective', *J Chester Archaeol Soc* 74 (1996-7) 63-87

M. Biddle 'Towns', in D.M. Wilson (ed.), *The Archaeology of Anglo-Saxon England* (Cambridge 1976), 99-150

M. Biddle and D. Hill 'Late Saxon planned towns', *Antiq J* 51 (1971) 70-85

J. Blair 'Palaces or minsters? Northampton and Cheddar reconsidered', *Anglo-Saxon England* 25 (1996) 97-121

J.D. Bullock 'The Celtic, Saxon and Scandinavian settlement at Meols, Wirral', *Trans Hist Soc Lancashire Cheshire* 112 (1960) 1-28

A. Carter 'The Anglo-Saxon origins of Norwich: the problems and approaches', *Anglo-Saxon England* 7 (1978) 175-204

H. Clarke and B. Ambrosiani *Towns in the Viking Age* (Leicester 1991)

C. Dallas 'Excavations in Thetford by B.K. Davison between 1964 and 1970' *East Anglian Archaeology* 62 (1992)

S. Dunmore and R. Carr 'The Late Saxon town of Thetford: an archaeological and historical survey', *East Anglian Archaeology* 4 (1976)

J. Gould 'First report on excavations at Tamworth, Staffs., 1967: The Saxon defences', *Trans Lichfield S Staffordshire Archaeol Hist Soc* 9 (1967) 17-29

J. Gould 'Third report on excavations at Tamworth, Staffs., 1968: The western entrance to the Saxon borough', *Trans Lichfield S Staffordshire Archaeol Hist Soc* 10 (1968) 32-43

A.R. Hall, H.K. Kenward, D. Williams, and J.R.A. Greig *Environment and living conditions at two Anglo-Scandinavian sites AY 14/4* (London 1983)

R.A. Hall 'The Pre-Conquest Burgh of Derby', *Derbyshire Archaeol J* 94 (1974) 16-23

R.A. Hall 'York 700-1050', in R. Hodges and B. Hobley (eds.) *The Rebirth of Towns in the West AD 700-1050 CBA Res Rep 68* (London 1988), 125-32

R.A. Hall 'The Five Boroughs of the Danelaw: a review of present knowledge', *Anglo-Saxon England* 18 (1989) 149-206

J. Haslam 'Market and fortress in England in the reign of Offa', *World Archaeology* 19 (1987) 76-93

J. Haslam (ed) *Anglo-Saxon Towns in Southern England* (Chichester 1984)

C.M. Heighway 'Anglo-Saxon Gloucester to AD 1000', in M. Faull (ed.) *Studies in Late Anglo-Saxon Settlement* (Oxford 1984) 35-53

C.M. Heighway *Anglo-Saxon Gloucestershire* (Gloucester 1987)

D.H. Hill 'The origins of the Saxon towns', in P. Brandon (ed.) *The South Saxons* (Chichester 1978) 174-89

C.M. Mahany 'Excavations in Stamford, Lincolnshire 1963-1969' *Soc Medieval Archaeol Monograph Ser 9* (London 1982)

C.M. Mahany and D. Roffe 'Stamford: the development of an Anglo-Scandinavian borough', *Anglo-Norman Stud* 5 (1983) 197-219

G. Milne 'Lundenwic to London town: from beach market to merchant port', *Arkeologiske Skrifter fra Historisk Museum, Universitetet i Bergen* 5 (1989)160-5

G. Milne and D. Goodburn 'The early medieval port of London AD 700-1200', *Antiquity* 64 (1990) 629-36

A.D. Morton (ed.) 'Excavations at Hamwic:Volume 1' *CBA Res Rep 84* (London 1992)

J. Moulden and D.Tweddle *Anglo-Scandinavian settlement south-west of the Ouse AY8/1* (London 1986)

D. Perring *Early Medieval occupation at Flaxengate, Lincoln ALIX-1* (London 1981)

C.A.R. Radford 'The later Pre-Conquest boroughs and their defences', *Medieval Archaeology* 14 (1970) 83-103

C.A.R. Radford 'The Pre-Conquest boroughs of England, ninth to eleventh centuries', *Proc Brit Acad* 64 (1978) 131-53

J. Radley 'Economic aspects of Anglo-Danish York', *Medieval Archaeology* 15 (1971) 37-58

P. Rahtz 'The archaeology of West Mercian towns', in A. Dornier (ed.) *Mercian Studies* (Leicester 1977), 107-29

A. Rogerson and C. Dallas 'Excavations at Thetford 1948-59 and 1973-80', *East Anglian Archaeology* 22 (1984)

C. Scull 'Urban centres in pre-Viking England?' in J. Hines (ed.) *The Anglo-Saxons from the Migration Period to the Eighth Century* (Woodbridge 1997), 269-310

K. Steedman,T. Dyson and J. Schofield 'Aspects of Saxo-Norman London: III.The bridgehead and Billingsgate to 1200' *London Middlesex Archaeol Soc Spec Paper* 14 (1992)

T. Tatton-Brown 'The Anglo-Saxon Towns of Kent', in D. Hooke (ed.), *Anglo-Saxon settlements* (Oxford 1988) 213-32

A.G.Vince *Saxon London: An archaeological investigation* (London 1990)

K. Wade 'Ipswich', in R. Hodges and B. Hobley (eds.) *The rebirth of towns in the West AD 700-1050 CBA Res Rep 68* (London 1988), 93-100

S. Ward *Excavations at Chester: Saxon occupation within the Roman fortress* (Chester 1994)

J.H. Williams *St Peter's Street, Northampton, Excavations 1973-1976* (Northampton 1979)

J.H. Williams 'A review of some aspects of Late Saxon urban origins and development', in M. Faull (ed.), *Studies in Late Anglo-Saxon settlement* (Oxford 1984) 25-34

J.H. Williams 'From 'palace' to 'town': Northampton and urban origins', *Anglo-Saxon England* 13 (1984) 113-36

5 THE BUILT ENVIRONMENT

C.E. Batey 'Aspects of rural settlement in Northern Britain', in D. Hooke and S. Burnell (eds.) *Landscape and settlement in Britain AD400-1066* (Exeter 1995) 69 94

G. Beresford 'Three deserted medieval settlements on Dartmoor', *Medieval Archaeology* 23 (1979) 98-158

R. Bruce-Mitford Mawgan 'Porth: a settlement of the late Saxon period on the north Cornish coast' *English Heritage Archaeol Report 13* (London 1997)

M.O.H. Carver 'Three Saxo-Norman tenements in Durham City', *Medieval Archaeology* 23 (1979) 1-80

D. Coggins, K.J. Fairless and C.E. Batey 'Simy Folds: An early medieval settlement in Upper Teesdale, Co Durham', *Medieval Archaeology* 27 (1983) 1-26

R.A. Hall 'Tenth century woodworking in Coppergate, York', in S. McGrail (ed.) *Woodworking techniques before AD 1500, Brit Archaeol Rep, (Int Ser), 129* (Oxford 1982) 231-44

R.A. Hall 'A late Pre-Conquest urban building tradition', in P. Addyman and V. Black (eds.) *Archaeological papers from York presented to M.W. Barley* (York 1984) 71-7

T. Hassall 'Archaeology of Oxford City', in G. Briggs, J. Cook and T. Rowley (eds.) *The Archaeology of the Oxford Region* (Oxford 1986) 115-34

V. Horsman, C. Milne and G. Milne 'Aspects of Saxo-Norman London: I. Building and street development London' *Middlesex Archaeol Soc Spec Paper 11* (1988)

P.J. Huggins 'The excavation of an eleventh-century Viking hall and fourteenth-century rooms at Waltham Abbey, Essex, 1969-71', *Medieval Archaeology 20* (1976) 75-133

A. King 'Gauber high pasture, Ribblehead – an interim report', in R.A. Hall (ed.) *Viking Age York and the North CBA Res Rep 27* (London 1978), 21-5

D.J.P. Mason 'Excavations at Chester: 26-42 Lower Bridge Street 1974-6: the Dark Age and Saxon Periods' *Grosvenor Museum Archaeological Excavation and Survey Reports 3* (Chester 1985)

G. Milne 'Timber building techniques in London c.900-1400' *London Middlesex Archaeol Soc Spec Paper 15* (1992)

D. O'Sullivan and R. Young *Lindisfarne: Holy Island* (London 1995)

P.A. Rahtz 'Buildings and rural settlement', in D.M. Wilson (ed.) *The Archaeology of Anglo-Saxon England* (Cambridge 1976), 49-98

J.D. Richards 'Identifying Anglo-Scandinavian settlements', in D. Hadley and J.D. Richards (eds.), 2000, 295-309

6 FEEDING THE PEOPLE

J. Clutton-Brock 'The animal resources', in D.M. Wilson (ed.) *The Archaeology of Anglo-Saxon England* (Cambridge 1976) 373-92

P.J. Fowler 'Agriculture and rural settlement', in D.M. Wilson (ed.) *The Archaeology of Anglo-Saxon England* (Cambridge 1976) 23-48

P.J. Fowler 'Farming in the Anglo-Saxon landscape', *Anglo-Saxon England 9* (1981) 263-80

M. Gardiner 'The exploitation of sea-mammals in medieval England: bones and their social context', *Archaeol J 154* (1997) 173-95

T.P. O'Connor *Animal Bones from Flaxengate, ALXVIII-1* (London 1982)

T.P. O'Connor *Bones from Anglo-Scandinavian Levels at 16-22 Coppergate, AY15/3* (London 1989)

T.P. O'Connor 'Eighth-eleventh century economy and environment
in York', in J. Rackham (ed.), *Environment and Economy in Anglo-
Saxon England, CBA Res Rep 89* (1994) 136-47

P. Rahtz and R. Meeson *An Anglo-Saxon watermill at Tamworth, CBA
Res Rep 83* (London 1992)

C. Salisbury 'The Trent, the story of a river', *Current Archaeology 74*
(1980) 88-91

7 CRAFT AND INDUSTRY

J. Bayley *Non-ferrous metalworking from Coppergate AY17/7* (London
1992)

L.A. Gilmour *Early medieval pottery from Flaxengate, Lincoln ALXVII-2*
(London 1988)

R.A. Hall *Viking Age York* (London 1994)

R. Hodges *The Anglo-Saxon achievement* (London 1989)

J.R. Hunter and M.P. Heyworth *The Hamwic glass, CBA Res Rep 116*
(York 1998)

J.G. Hurst 'The pottery', in D.M. Wilson (ed.) *The Archaeology of
Anglo-Saxon England* (Cambridge 1976) 283-348

E.M. Jope 'The Saxon building-stone industry in southern and
midland England', *Medieval Archaeology 8* (1964) 91-118

K. Kilmurry *The pottery industry of Stamford, Lincolnshire, c.AD 850-
1250, Brit Archaeol Rep (Brit Ser), 84* (Oxford 1980)

G. McDonnell 'Iron and its alloys in the fifth to eleventh centuries
AD in England', *World Archaeology 20* (1989) 373-82

A. MacGregor *Anglo-Scandinavian finds from Lloyds Bank, Pavement and
other sites AY17/3* (London 1982)

A. MacGregor *Bone, antler, ivory and horn* (London 1985)

A. MacGregor, A. Mainman, and N. Rogers *Craft, industry and
everyday life: Bone, antler, ivory and horn from Anglo-Scandinavian and
Medieval York AY17/12* (York 1999)

A. Mainman *Anglo-Scandinavian pottery from 16-22 Coppergate AY16/5*
(London 1990)

J.E. Mann *Early medieval finds from Flaxengate I: Objects of antler, bone,
stone, horn, ivory, amber, and jet ALXIV-1* (London 1982)

S. Margeson *The Vikings in Norfolk* (Norwich 1997)

M. Mellor 'Late Saxon pottery from Oxfordshire: evidence and speculation', *Medieval Ceramics* 4 (1980) 17-27

G. Milne 'Timber building techniques in London c.900-1400', *London Middlesex Archaeol Soc Spec Paper* 15 (1992)

C.A. Morris 'A Late Saxon hoard of iron and copper-alloy artefacts from Nazeing, Essex', *Medieval Archaeology* 27 (1983) 27-39

P.J. Ottaway *Anglo-Scandinavian ironwork from Coppergate AY17/6* (London 1992)

F.A. Pritchard 'Late Saxon textiles from the City of London', *Medieval Archaeology* 28 (1984) 46-76

G. Thomas 'Scandinavian metalwork in the Danelaw: reconstructing social interaction and regional identities' in D. Hadley and J.D. Richards (eds.), 2000, 237-55

D. Tweddle *Finds from Parliament Street and other sites in the city centre AY17/4* (London 1986)

A.G. Vince 'The Saxon and medieval pottery of London: a review', *Medieval Archaeology* 29 (1985) 25-93

A.G. Vince 'Aspects of Saxo-Norman London: II. Finds and environmental evidence', *London Middlesex Archaeol Soc Spec Paper* 12 (1991)

P. Walton *Textiles, cordage and raw fibre from 16-22 Coppergate, AY17/5* (London 1989)

P. Walton *Rogers Textile production at 16-22 Coppergate, AY17/11* (York 1997)

D. Williams *Late Saxon stirrup-strap mounts, CBA Res Rep 111* (York 1997)

8 TRADE AND EXCHANGE

M.A.S. Blackburn 'Coin finds and coin circulation in Lindsay, c.600-900, in A.G. Vince (ed.) *Pre-Viking Lindsey*, Lincoln Archaeological Studies 1 (Lincoln 1993) 80-90

M. Dolley 'The coins', in D.M. Wilson (ed.) *The Archaeology of Anglo-Saxon England* (Cambridge 1976) 349-72

M. Dolley 'The Anglo-Danish and Anglo-Norse coinages of York', in R.A. Hall (ed.), *Viking Age York and the North CBA Res Rep 27* (London 1978) 26-31

V. Fenwick (ed.) 'The Graveney Boat: a tenth-century find from Kent', *Brit Archaeol Re (Brit Ser)* 53 (Oxford 1978)

D.A. Hinton 'Coins and commercial centres in Anglo-Saxon England', in M.A.S. Blackburn (ed.) *Anglo-Saxon monetary history: Essays in memory of Michael Dolley* (Leicester 1986) 11-26

D. Hurst (ed.) *A multi-period salt production site at Droitwich: excavations at Upwich, CBA Res Rep 107* (York 1997)

H.K. Kenward and A.R. Hall *Biological evidence from 16-22 Coppergate, AY 14/7* (York 1995)

S. McGrail (ed) 'Logboats of England and Wales', *Brit Archaeol Rep (Brit Ser)* 51 (Oxford 1978)

S. McGrail and R. Switsur 'Medieval logboats of the River Mersey — a classificatory survey', in S. McGrail (ed.) *The archaeology of ships and harbours in Northern Europe, Brit Archaeol Rep (Int Ser)* 66 (Oxford 1979) 93-115

P. Marsden *et al.* 'A late Saxon logboat from Clapton, London Borough of Hackney', *Int J Naut Archaeol Underwater Explor* 18 (1989) 89-111

D. Pelteret 'Slave raiding and slave trading in early England', *Anglo-Saxon England* 9 (1981) 99-114

E.J.E. Pirie *Post-Roman coins from York excavations 1971-81, AY 18/1* (London 1986)

H. Sarfatij 'Tiel in succession to Dorestad' in H. Sarfatij, W.J.H. Verwers, and P.J. Woltering (eds.) *In discussion with the past: archaeological studies presented to W.A. van Es* (Zwolle 1999) 267-78

P.H. Sawyer 'Anglo-Scandinavian trade in the Viking Age and after', in M.A.S. Blackburn (ed.) *Anglo-Saxon monetary history: essays in memory of Michael Dolley* (Leicester 1986) 185-99

P. Walton *Textiles, cordage and raw fibre from 16-22 Coppergate, AY 17/5* (London 1989)

S. Ward *Excavations at Chester: Saxon occupation within the Roman fortress* (Chester 1994)

9 CHURCHES AND MONASTERIES

P. Armstrong, D. Tomlinson and D.H. Evans 'Excavations at Lurk Lane Beverley, 1979-82', *Sheffield Excavation Reports* 1 (Sheffield 1991)

R.D. Bell, M.W. Beresford *et al.* 'Wharram Percy: The Church of St Martin Wharram: A Study of Settlement on the Yorkshire Wolds Volume III', *Soc Medieval Archaeol Monograph Ser 11* (London 1987)

J. Blair 'Minster churches in the landscape', in D. Hooke (ed.), *Anglo-Saxon settlements* (Oxford 1988) 35–58

J. Blair 'Bampton: an Anglo-Saxon minster', *Current Archaeology* 14 (1998) 124–30

A. Boddington 'Raunds Furnells: The Anglo-Saxon church and churchyard', *English Heritage Archaeological Report 7* (London 1996)

R. Gem 'The English parish church in the eleventh and early twelfth centuries: A Great Rebuilding?', in J. Blair (ed.) *Minsters and parish churches. The local church in transition* (Oxford 1988), 21–30

B.J. Gilmour and D.A. Stocker *St Mark's Church and Cemetery, ALXIII-1* (London 1986)

J. Magilton *The Church of St Helen-on-the-Walls, Aldwark, AY10/1* (London 1980)

R.K. Morris *Churches in the landscape* (London 1989)

C.A.R. Radford 'Pre-conquest minster churches', *Archaeol J* 130 (1973) 120–40

P. Rahtz and L. Watts *Kirkdale Archaeology 1996-1997* (Helmsley 1998)

J. Wall 'Anglo-Saxon sundials in Ryedale', *Yorkshire Archaeol J* 69 (1997) 93–117

L. Watts, P. Rahtz, E. Okasha, S.A.J. Bradley, and J. Higgitt 'Kirkdale — the inscriptions', *Medieval Archaeology* 41 (1997) 51–99

W.J. White 'Skeletal remains from the cemetery of St Nicholas Shambles', *London Middlesex Archaeol Soc Spec Paper 9* (1988)

10 DEATH AND BURIAL

M. Adams 'Excavation of a pre-Conquest Cemetery at Addingham, West Yorkshire', *Medieval Archaeology* 40 (1996) 151–191

M.L. Alexander 'A "Viking-Age" grave from Cambois, Bedlington, Northumberland', *Medieval Archaeology* 31 (1987) 101–5

M. Biddle and J. Blair 'The Hook Norton hoard of 1848: a Viking burial from Oxfordshire?', *Oxoniensia* 52 (1987) 186–95

M. Biddle and B. Kjølbye-Biddle 'Repton and the Vikings', *Antiquity* 66 (1992) 36–51

J. Blair and B.E. Crawford 'A late-Viking burial at Magdalen Bridge, Oxford?', *Oxoniensia* 62 (1997) 135-43

A. Boddington 'Raunds Furnells: The Anglo-Saxon church and churchyard', *English Heritage Archaeological Report* 7 (London 1996)

J.D. Cowen 'Viking burials in Cumbria', *Trans Cumberland Westmorland Antiq Archaeol Soc NS 48* (1948) 73-6

J.D. Cowen 'Viking burials in Cumbria – a supplement', *Trans Cumberland Westmorland Antiq Archaeol Soc NS 67* (1967) 31-4

M.J. Darling and D.J. Gurney 'Caister-on-Sea excavations by Charles Green, 1951-55', *East Anglian Archaeology* 60 (1993)

B.J.N. Edwards *Vikings in North West England: The Artifacts* (Lancaster 1998)

F. Elgee *Early Man in North-East Yorkshire* (Gloucester 1930)

V.I. Evison 'A Viking grave at Sonning, Berks', *Antiq J* 49 (1969) 330-45

R.A. Hall 'A silver appliqué from St Mary Bishophill', *Yorks Arch J* 70 (1997) 61-6

R.A. Hall and M. Whyman 'Settlement and monasticism at Ripon, North Yorkshire, from the seventh to eleventh centuries AD', *Medieval Archaeology* 40 (1996) 62-150

G. Halsall 'The Viking presence in England? The burial evidence reconsidered' in D. Hadley and J.D. Richards (eds.), 2000, 259-76

P.J. Huggins 'A note on a Viking-style plate from Waltham Abbey, Essex and its implications for a disputed Late-Viking building', *Archaeol J* 141 (1984) 175-81

P.J. Huggins 'Excavation on the north side of Sun Street, Waltham Abbey, Essex, 1974-75: Saxon burials, precinct wall and south-east transept', *Essex Archaeol Hist* 19 (1988) 117-53

G. Keevill *Carlisle Cathedral excavations 1988: interim report* (Carlisle 1989)

S. Margeson *The Vikings in Norfolk* (Norwich 1997)

D. Philips and B. Heywood *Excavations at York Minster Volume I: Roman to Norman* (London 1995)

M. Posnansky 'The pagan-Danish barrow cemetery at Heath Wood, Ingleby', *Derbyshire Archaeol J* 76 (1956) 40-56

T.W. Potter and R.D. Andrews 'Excavation and survey at St Patrick's Chapel and St Peter's Church, Heysham, Lancashire, 1977-8', *Antiq J* 74 (1994) 55-134

J.D. Richards, with M. Jecock, L. Richmond and C. Tuck 'The Viking
barrow cemetery at Heath Wood, Ingleby, Derbyshire', *Medieval
Archaeology* 39 (1995) 51-70

W. Rodwell and K. Rodwell 'St Peter's church, Barton-upon-
Humber: excavation and structural study, 1978-81', *Antiq J* 62
(1982) 283-315

H. Shetelig *Viking Antiquities in Great Britain and Ireland, vol IV* (Oslo
1940)

R. Shoesmith *Hereford City excavations, Vol 1. Excavations at Castle
Green, CBA Res Rep 36* (London 1980)

L.P. Wenham, R.A. Hall, C.M. Briden, and D.A. Stocker *St Mary
Bishophill Junior and St Mary Castlegate, AY8/2* (London 1987)

11 MONUMENTS IN STONE

R.N. Bailey *Viking Age sculpture in northern England* (London 1980)

P. Everson and D. Stocker *Corpus of Anglo-Saxon stone sculpture Vol V,
Lincolnshire* (Oxford 1999)

B. Kjølbye-Biddle and R.I. Page 'A Scandinavian rune-stone from
Winchester', *Antiq J* 55 (1975) 389-94

J.T. Lang 'Anglo-Scandinavian sculpture in Yorkshire', in R.A. Hall
(ed.) *Viking Age York and the North, CBA Res Rep 27* (London
1978) 11-20

J.T. Lang 'The hogback: a Viking colonial monument', *Anglo-Saxon
Stud Archaeol Hist* 3 (1984) 85-176

J.T. Lang *Anglo-Saxon sculpture* (Princes Risborough 1988)

J.T. Lang *Corpus of Anglo-Saxon stone sculpture Vol III, York and eastern
Yorkshire* (Oxford 1991)

R.I. Page *Runes: reading the past* (London 1987)

R.I. Page *An introduction to English runes* (Woodbridge 1999) 2nd ed.

P. Sidebottom 'Viking Age stone monuments and social identity', in
D. Hadley and J.D. Richards (eds.), 2000, 213-35

D. Stocker 'Monuments and merchants: irregularities in the distribution of stone sculpture in Lincolnshire and Yorkshire in the tenth
century', in D. Hadley and J.D. Richards (eds.), 2000, 179-212

D.A. Walsh 'Ryedale zoomorphic ornament and tenth-century
Anglo-Scandinavian art' *J Brit Archaeol Assoc* 147 (1994) 9-35

INDEX

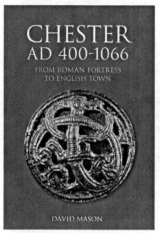

Chester AD 400–1066
From Roman Fortress to English Town

David Mason

978 0 7524 4100 9   £17.99

This is the most up-to-date general account of Chester from the late Roman period to the Norman Conquest. Its author tells the story of Chester; its disappearance into obscurity during the 'Dark Ages', its emergence as an important religious, commercial and military settlement in the Kingdom of Mercia and the everyday life of its people leading up to the advent of Norman rule.

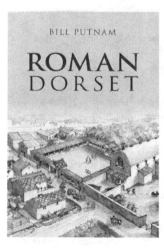

Roman Dorset

Bill Putnam

978 0 7524 4104 7   £17.99

At the time of the Roman invasion present-day Dorset was part of the territory of the Durotriges. The Second Legion Augusta was responsible for the conquest of this area and Bill Putnam charts the remarkable extent to which Roman ideas, life and language were adopted in the years following this conquest. This book is the result of 40 years of fieldwork and research by the author.

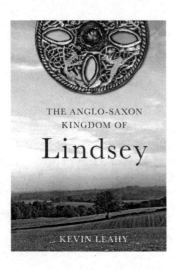

The Anglo-Saxon Kingdom of Lindsey

Kevin Leahy

978 0 7524 4111 5   £19.99

Lindsey was a small Anglo-Saxon kingdom that lay to the south of the Humber Estuary. Over the last 50 years, this kingdom has emerged from its own 'dark age' to reappear as a highly prosperous and sophisticated area that was on the edge of great events with a flourishing Christian culture until the Viking invasion of AD 877.

The Late Anglo-Saxon Army

I.P. Stephenson

978 0 7524 3141 3   £17.99

As a result of the Battle of Hastings the late Anglo-Saxon army has had a bad press, more famous for its defeats than its victories. In this study the author looks at the history, organisation, tactics and equipment of the army and argues that rather than being a failure, the late Anglo-Saxon army was not only adaptive, but also innovative, and doesn't deserve its rather dubious reputation.

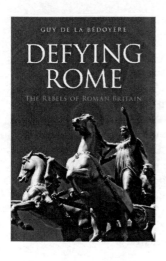

Defying Rome
The Rebels of Roman Britain

Guy de la Bédoyère

978 0 7524 4440 6   £17.99

Rome's power was under constant challenge
and nowhere moreso than in Britain. From
the beginning to the end of Roman rule in
Britain a succession of idealists and chancers,
most famously Boudica, tried to expel Rome
and recover their lost power. This book covers
14 rebellions and explains why Britain was
such a hot-bed of dissent.

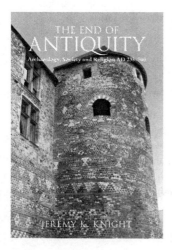

The End of Antiquity
Archaeology, Society and Religion AD
235-700

Jeremy K. Knight

978 0 7524 4082 8   £17.99

This is a masterful study of the transition from
the Classical world to Medieval Europe and
has won widespread critical acclaim.

'For this well written, well illsutrated and
scholarly book, he has placed all students of
Late Antiquity in his debt' - *Antiquaries Journal*

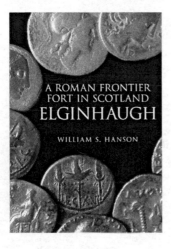

A Roman Frontier Fort in Scotland
Elginhaugh

William S. Hanson

978 0 7524 4113 9   £17.99

Elginhaugh is the only completely excavated timber-built auxiliary fort in the Roman Empire. Here the excavator, Prof. W.S. Hanson tells the story of its discovery and excavation, interprets the evidence and discusses the nature of military life on the furthest northern frontier of the Empire in the first century AD and its impact on the local area.

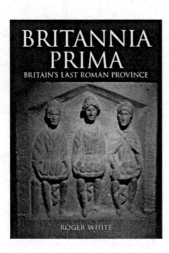

Britannia Prima
Britain's Last Roman Province

Roger White

978 0 7524 1967 1   £19.99

This important work counters the widely held view that when the legions left Britain the Roman way of life disappeared with them. In fact Britannia Prima – broadly the west of Britain – had from the fourth to the sixth centuries a distinctive Romano-British character and successfully resisted significant Anglo-Saxon invasion longer than any other area of Britain.

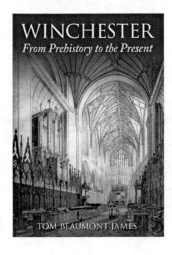

Winchester
From Prehistory to Present

Tom Beaumont James

978 0 7524 3742 2   £17.99

The story of Winchester is both chequered
and colourful. Tom Beaumont James takes the
reader on a fascinating journey through the
history of this great city, from its beginnings as
a pre-Roman tribal centre, through its roles as
Anglo-Saxon capital and its decimation by the
Black Death, to its dramatic revival in the age
of steam.

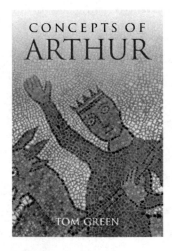

Concepts of Arthur

Tom Green
978 0 7524 4461 1   £18.99

Ever since the 12th century there has been
an effort to show that the Arthur of Celtic
legend was based on an historical figure. In
this re-examination of all the early literature
Tom Green argues that far from being an
historical figure mythicized, Arthur emerges as
a mythical and/or folkloric figure historicized.
Looking at the latest research into Celtic and
Indo-European deities, the author concludes
with the suggestion that Arthur may well
have been a local deity, the product of a pre-
Christian mythology.

If you are interested in purchasing other books published by The History Press, or in case you have difficulty finding any of our books in your local bookshop, you can also place orders directly through our website.

www.thehistorypress.co.uk